AF413578

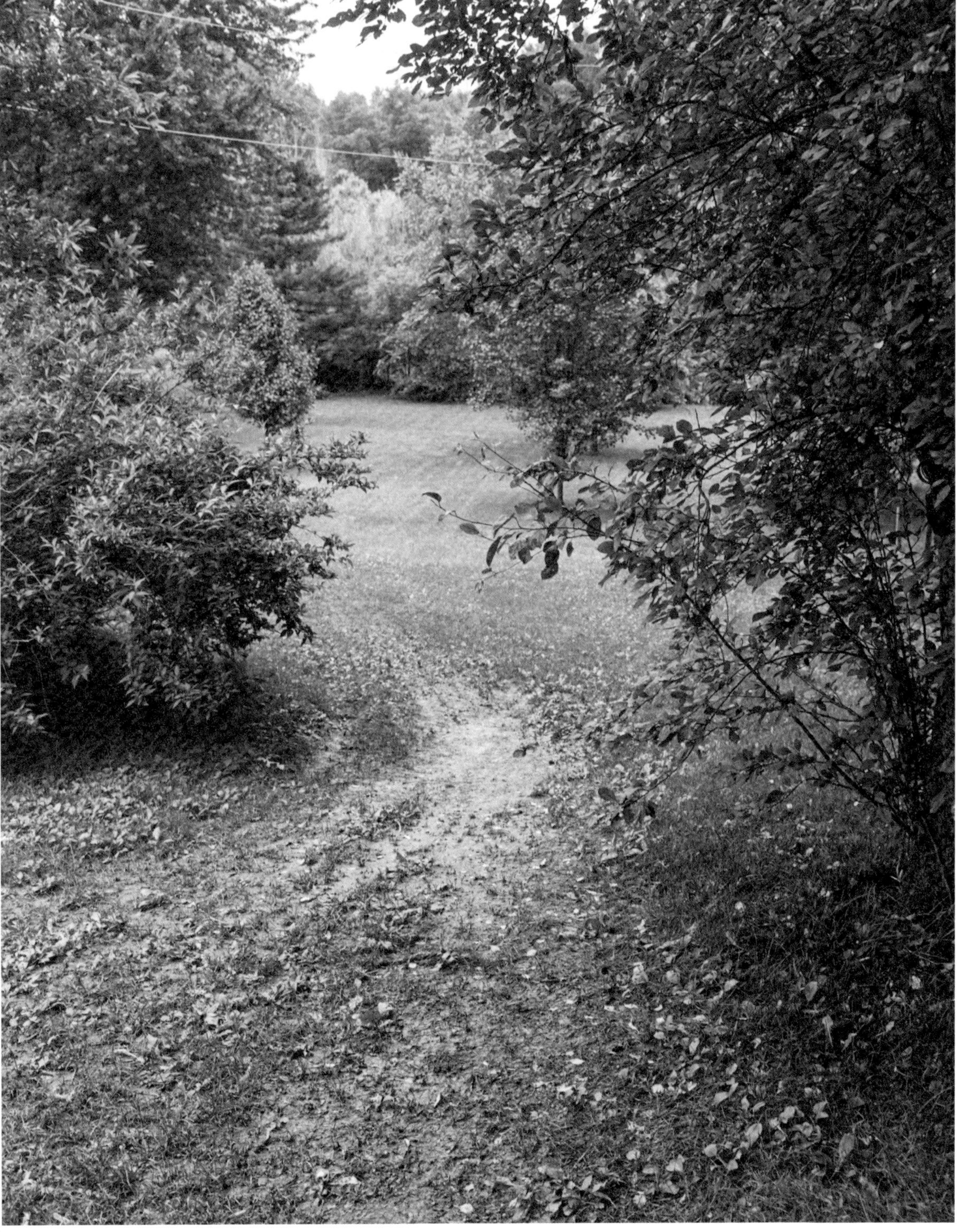

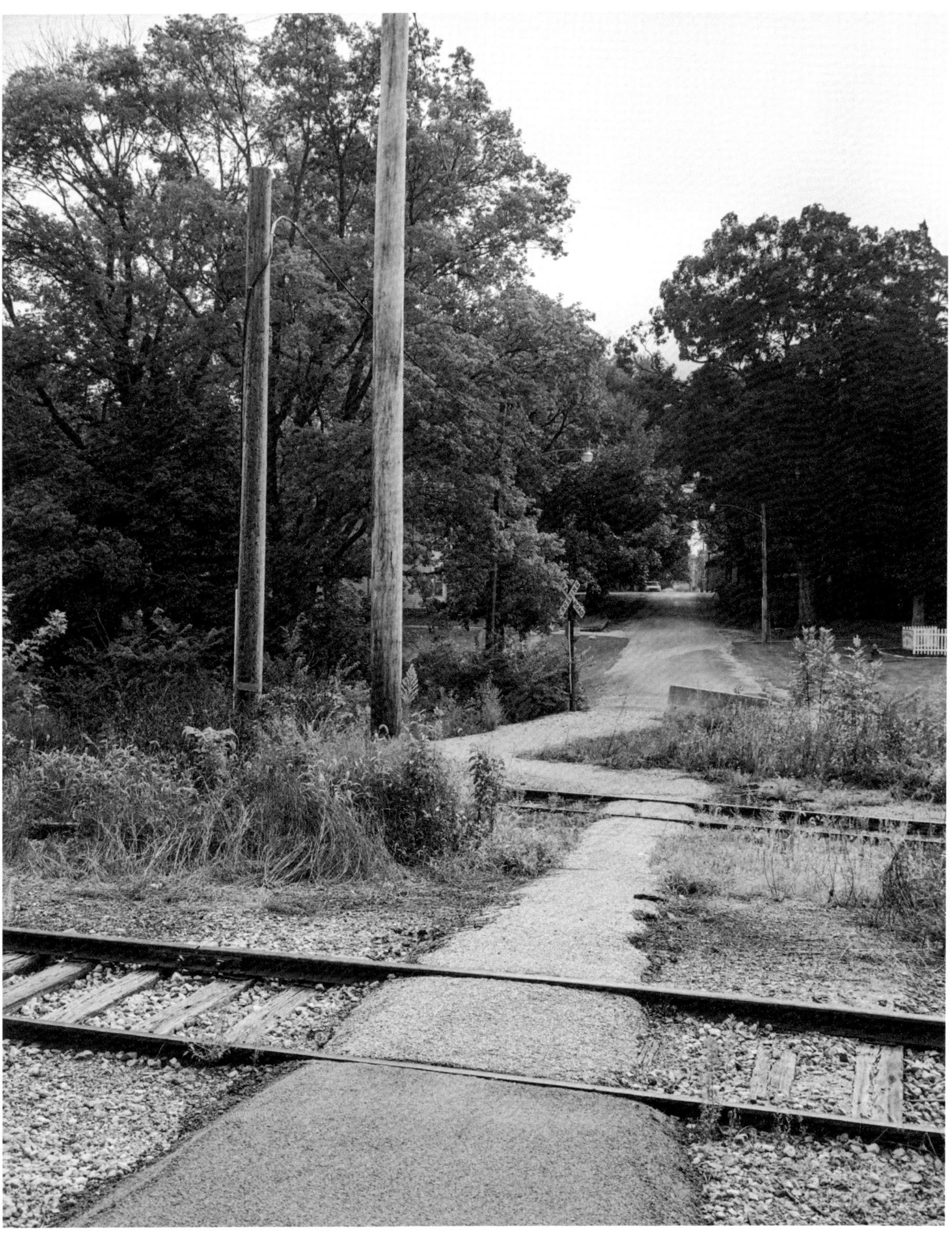

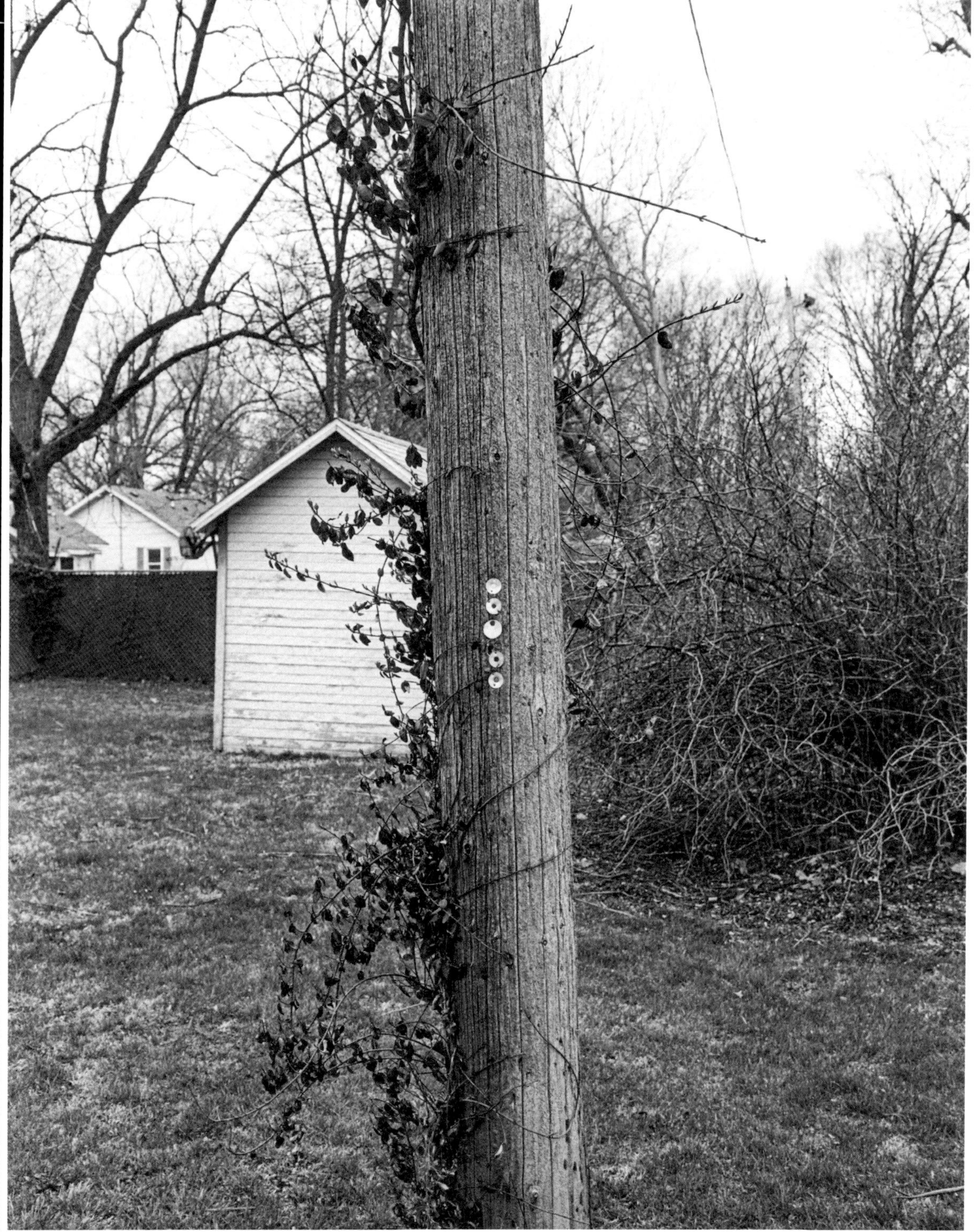

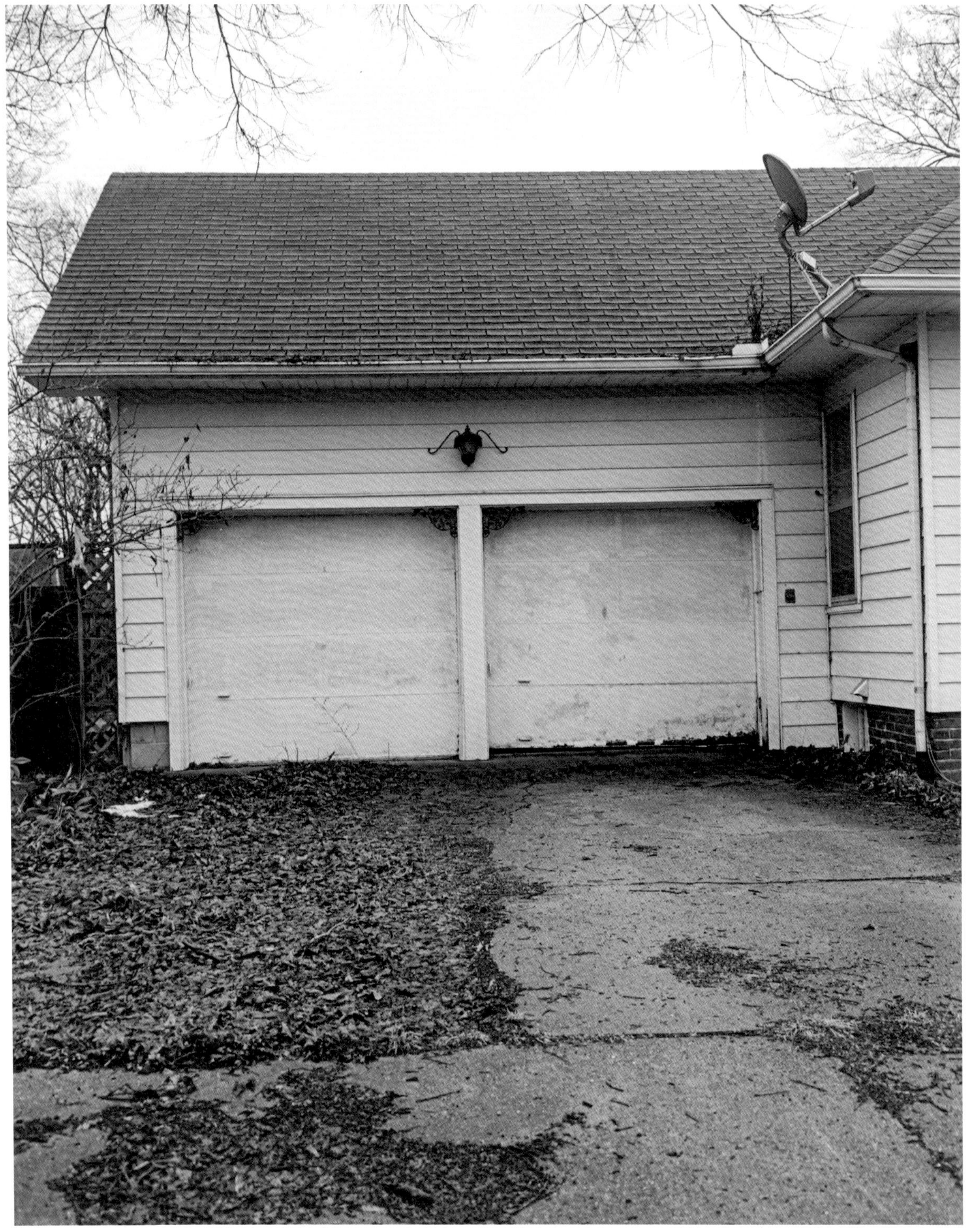

Little

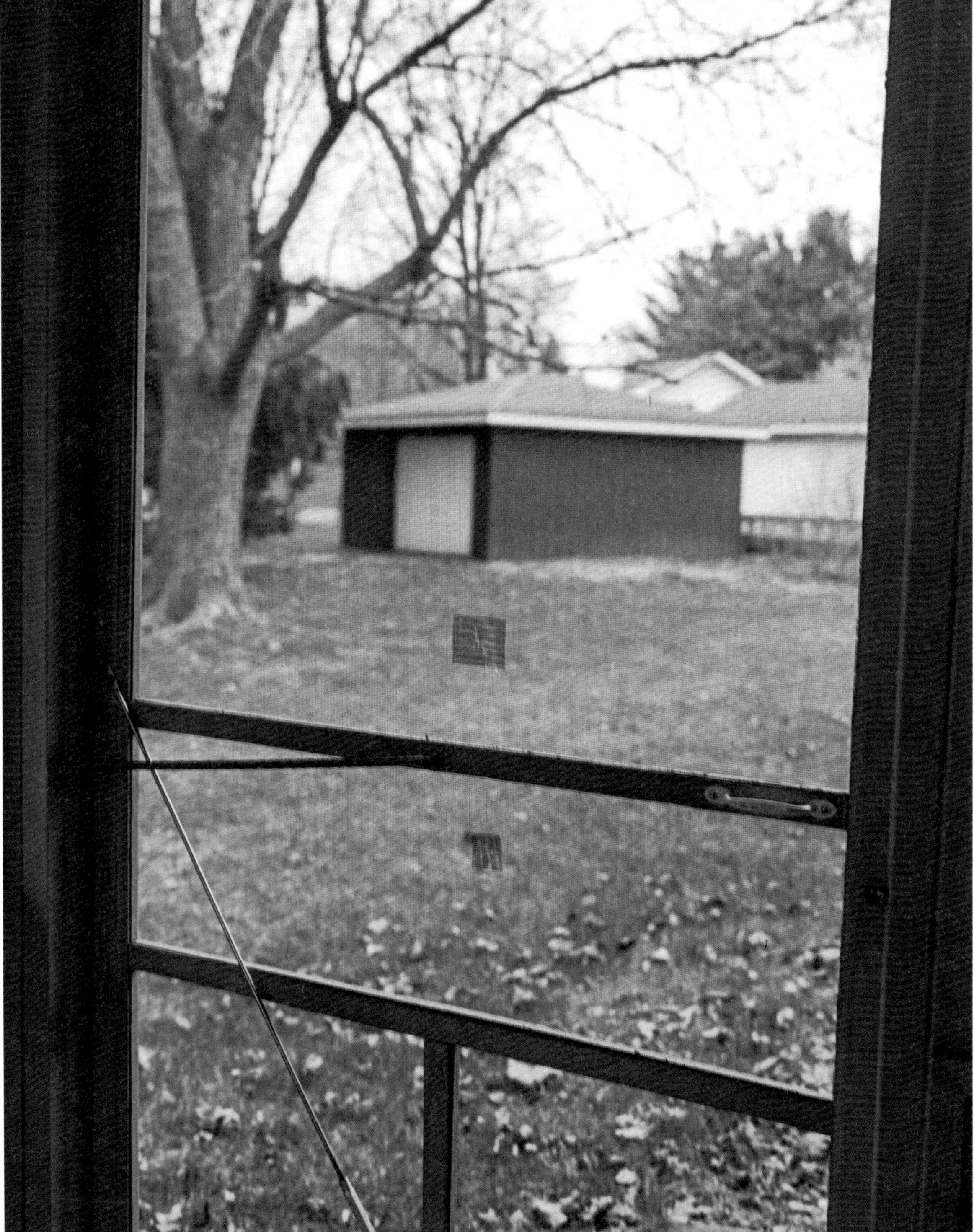

(song for Vic Chesnutt)

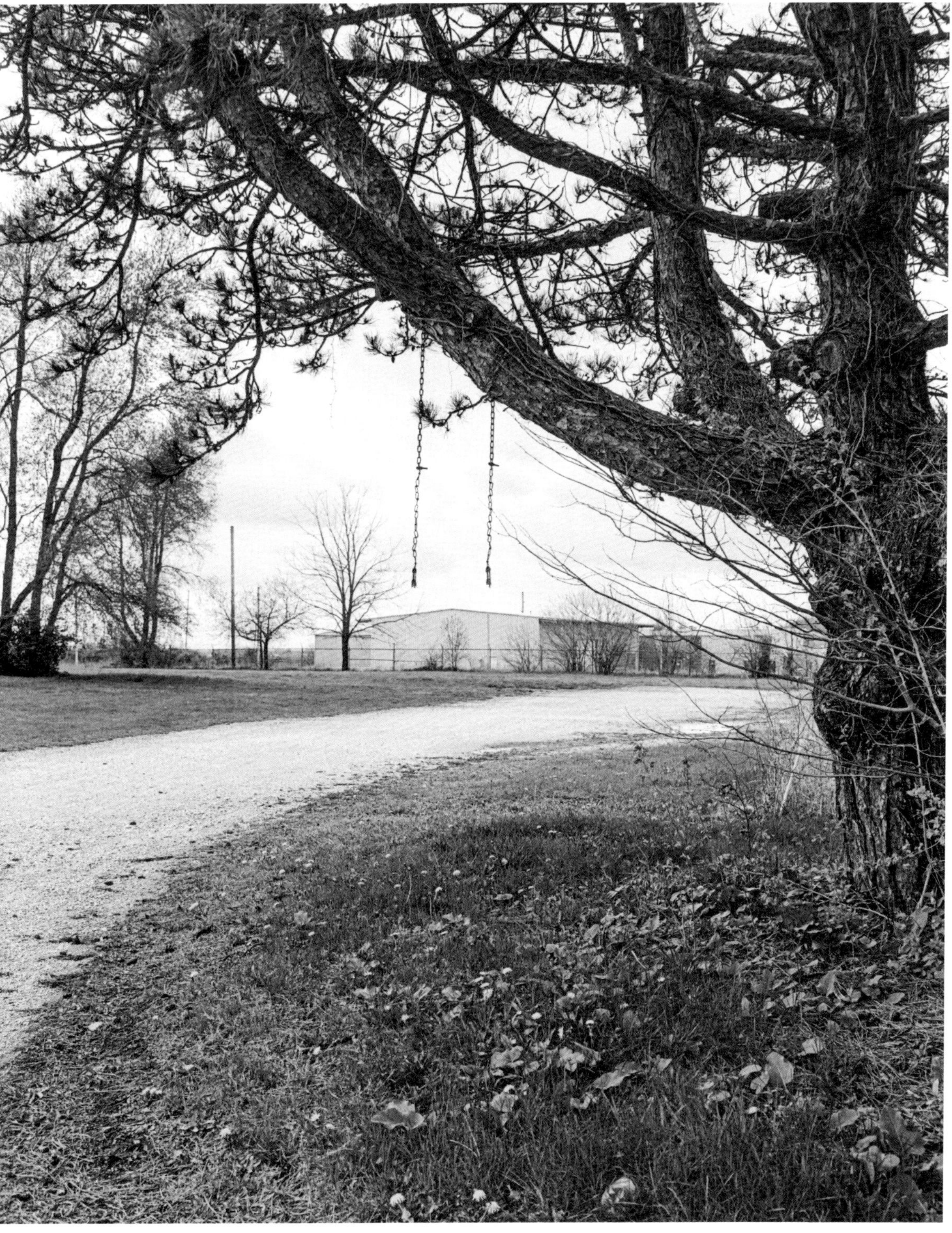

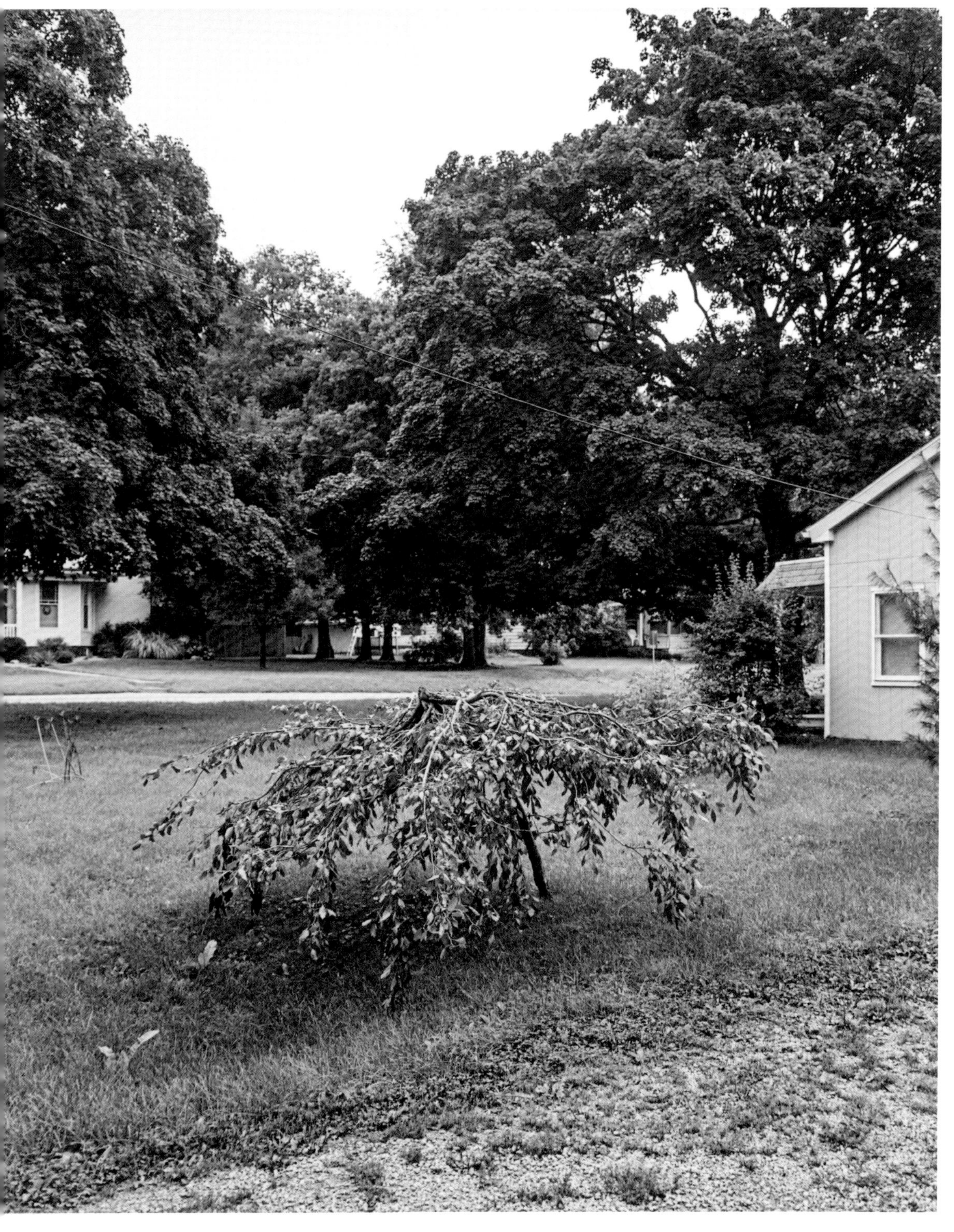

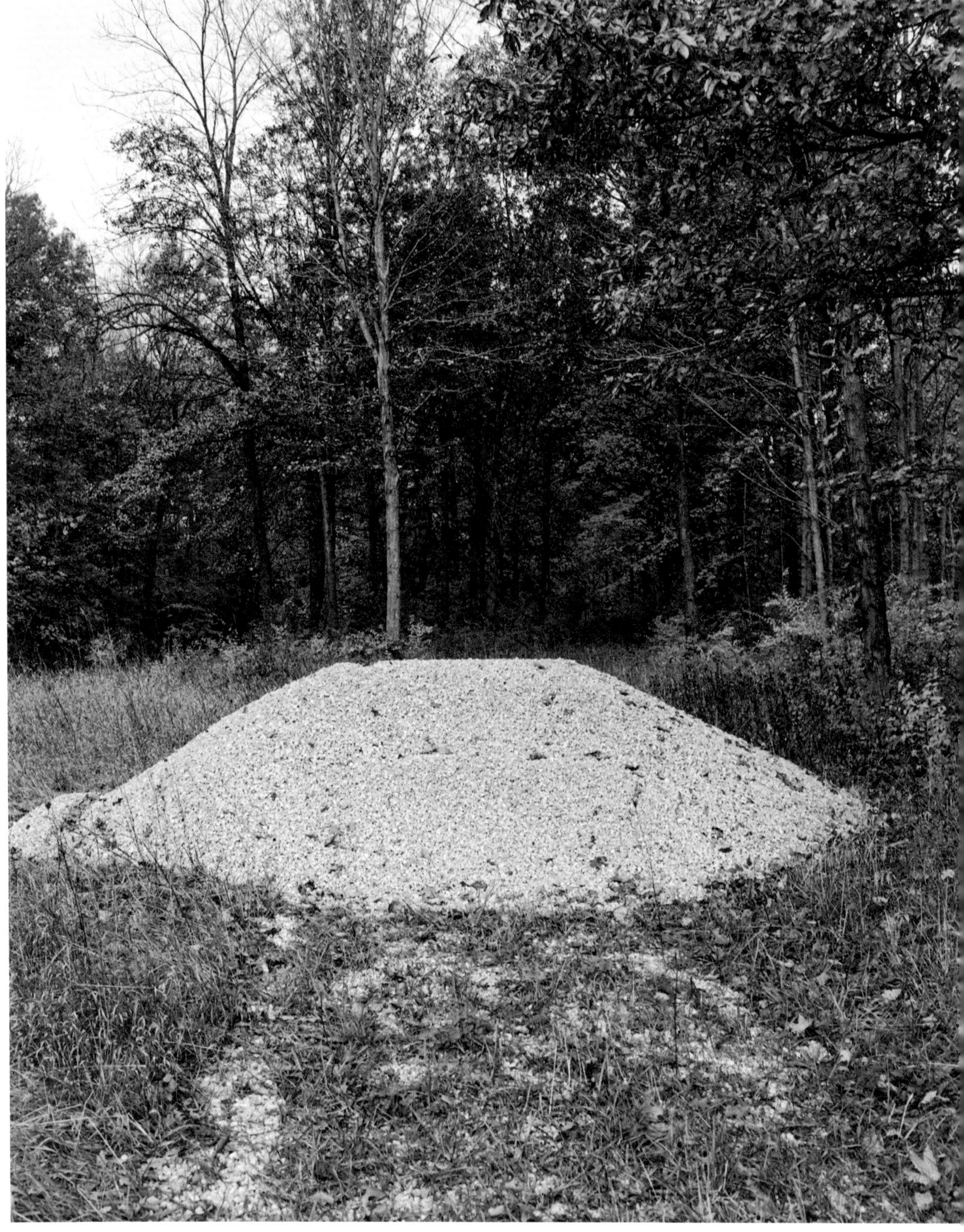

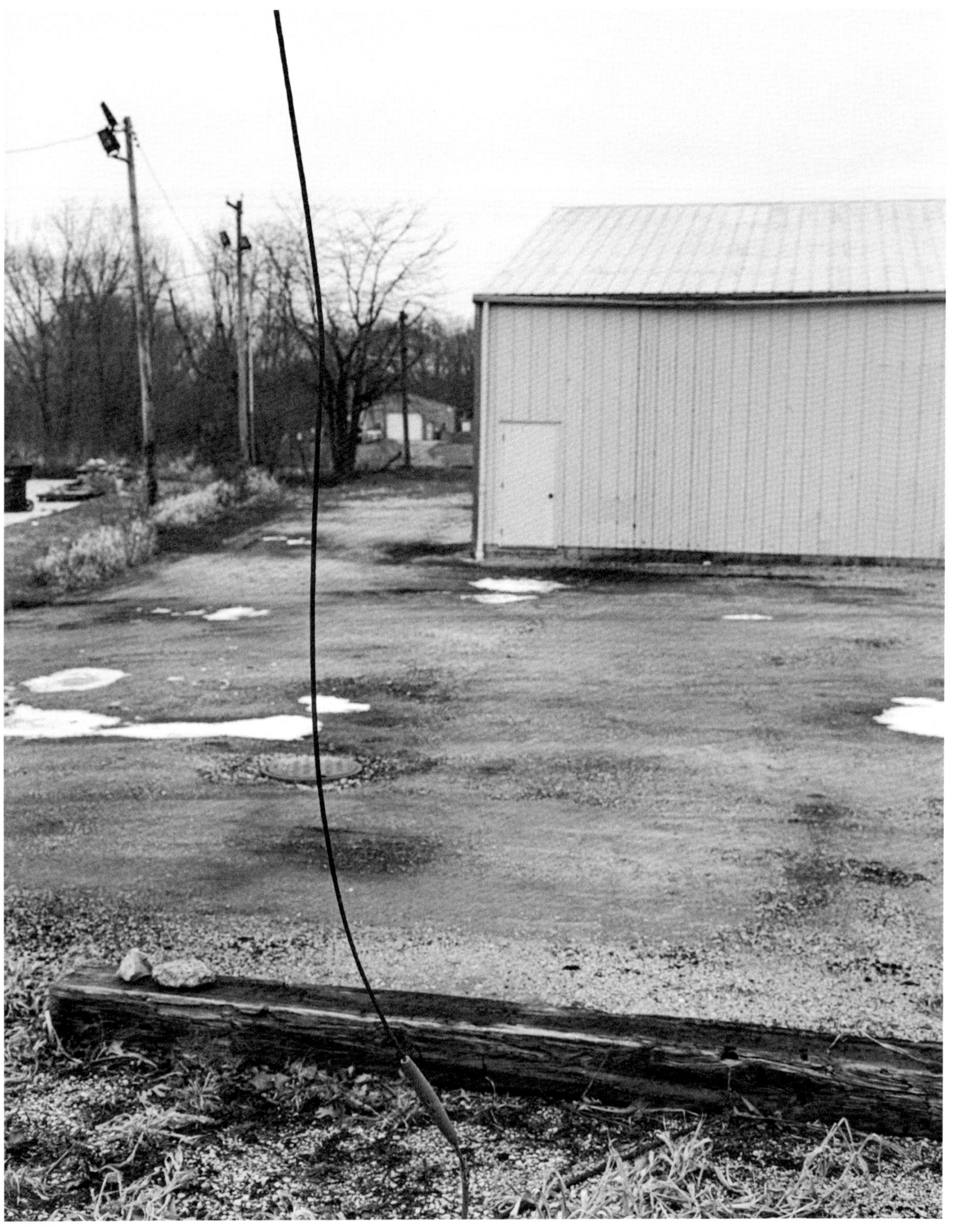

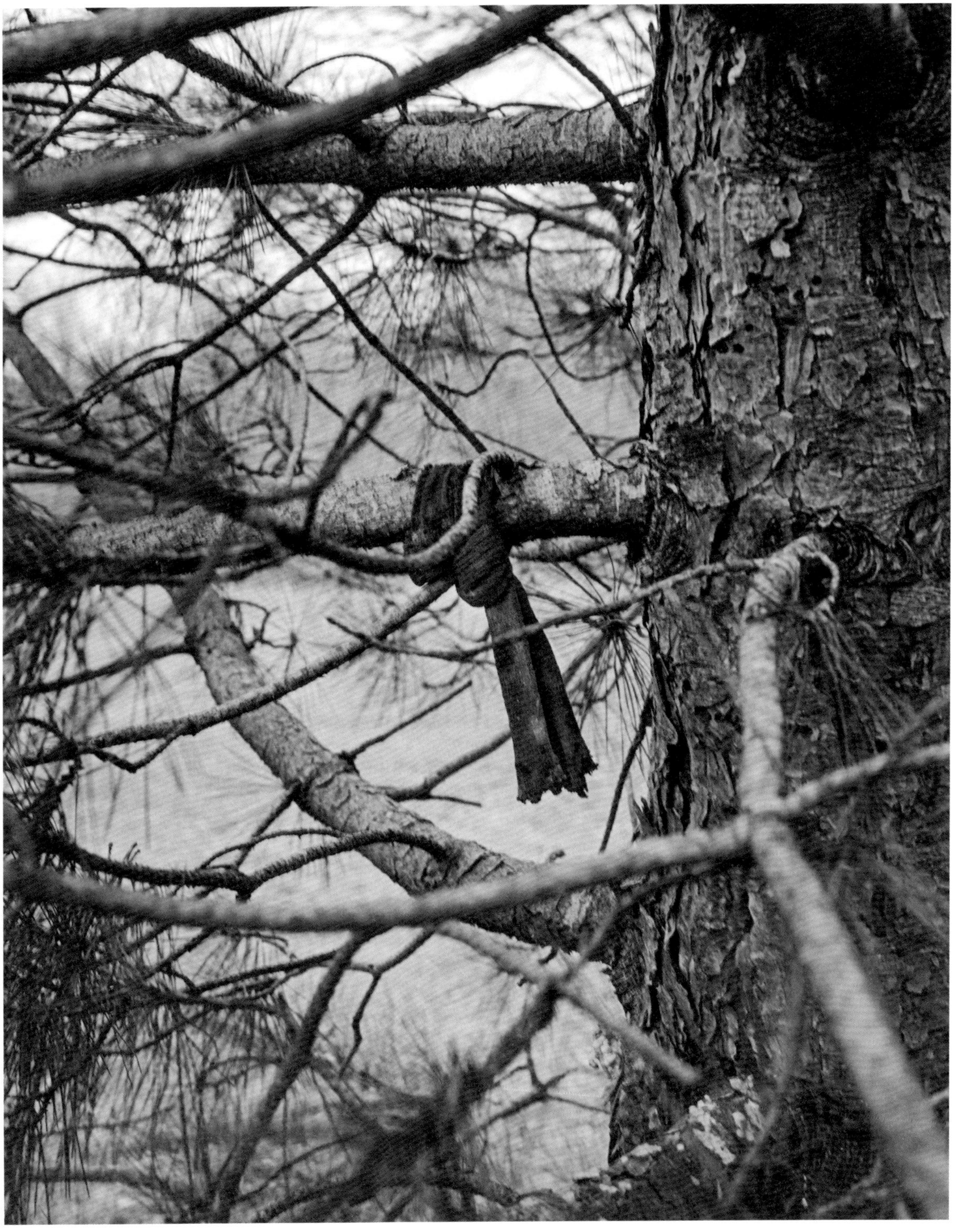

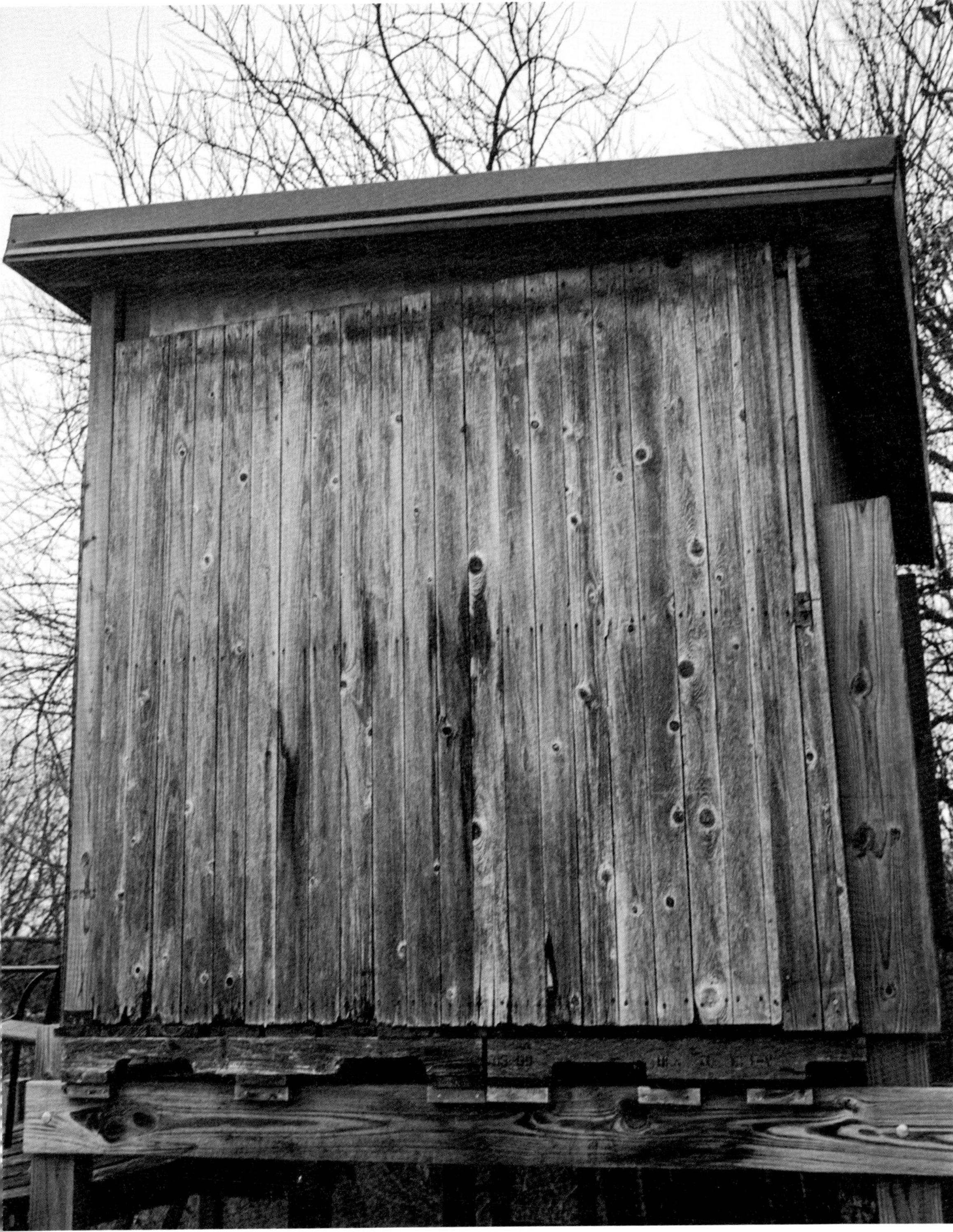

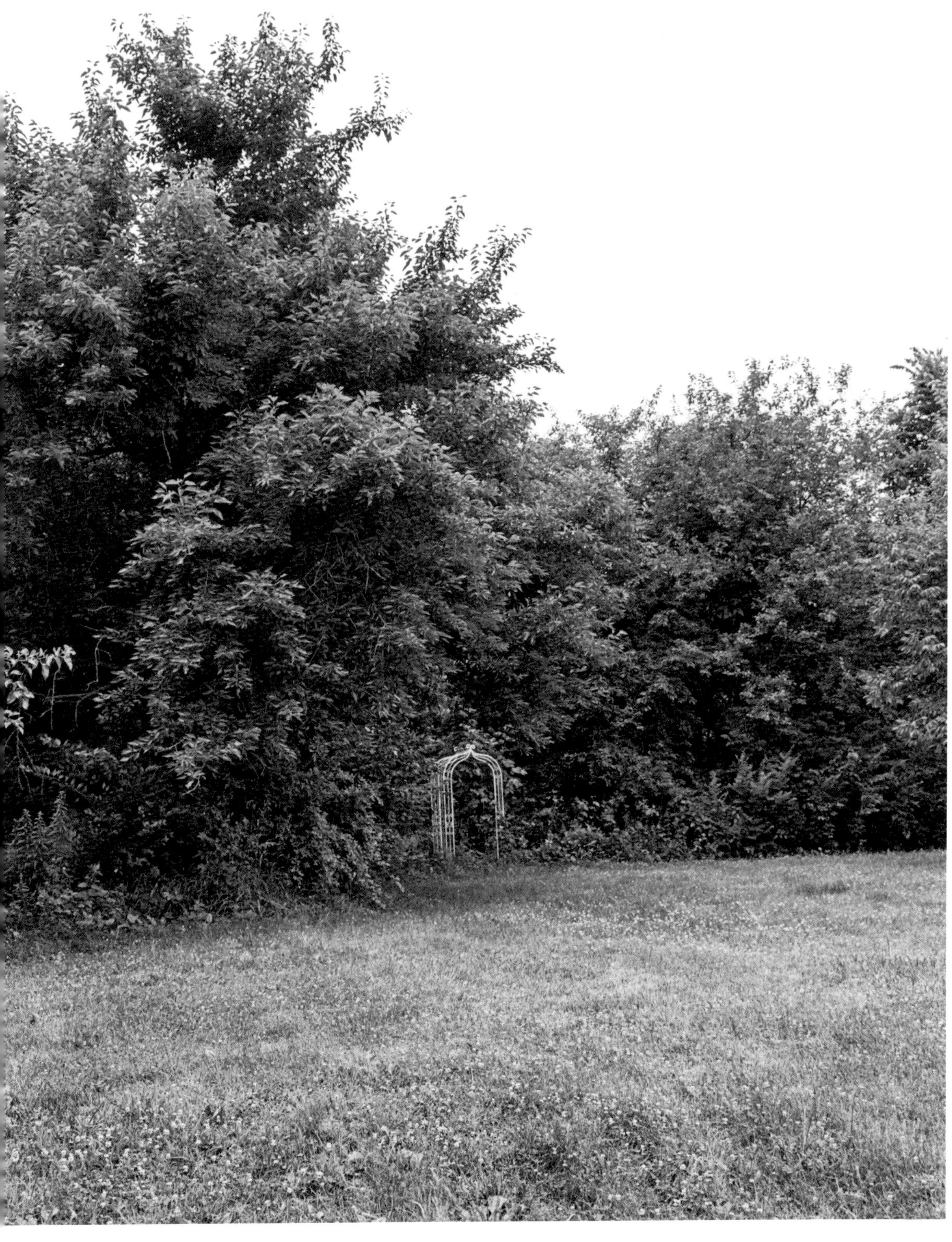

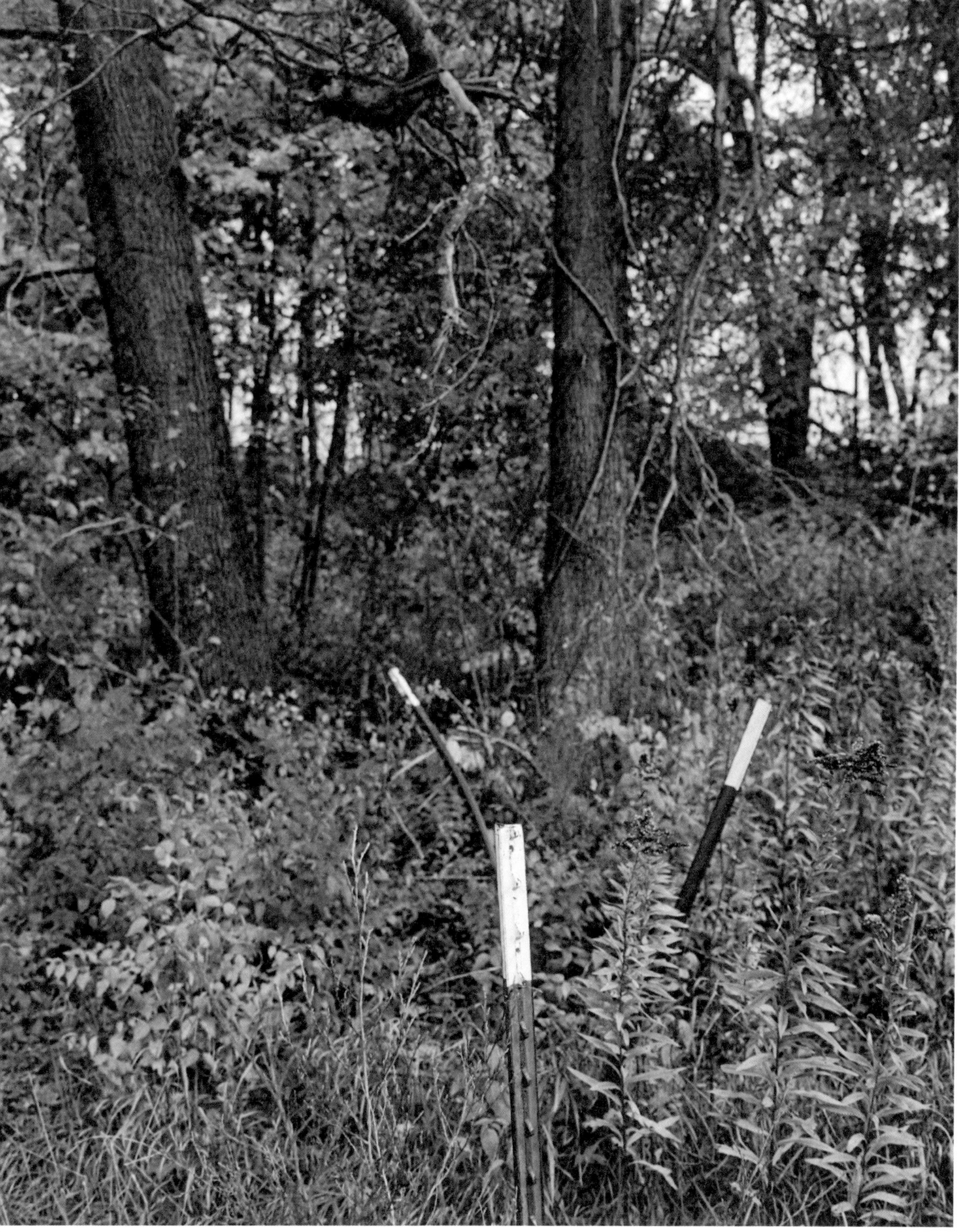

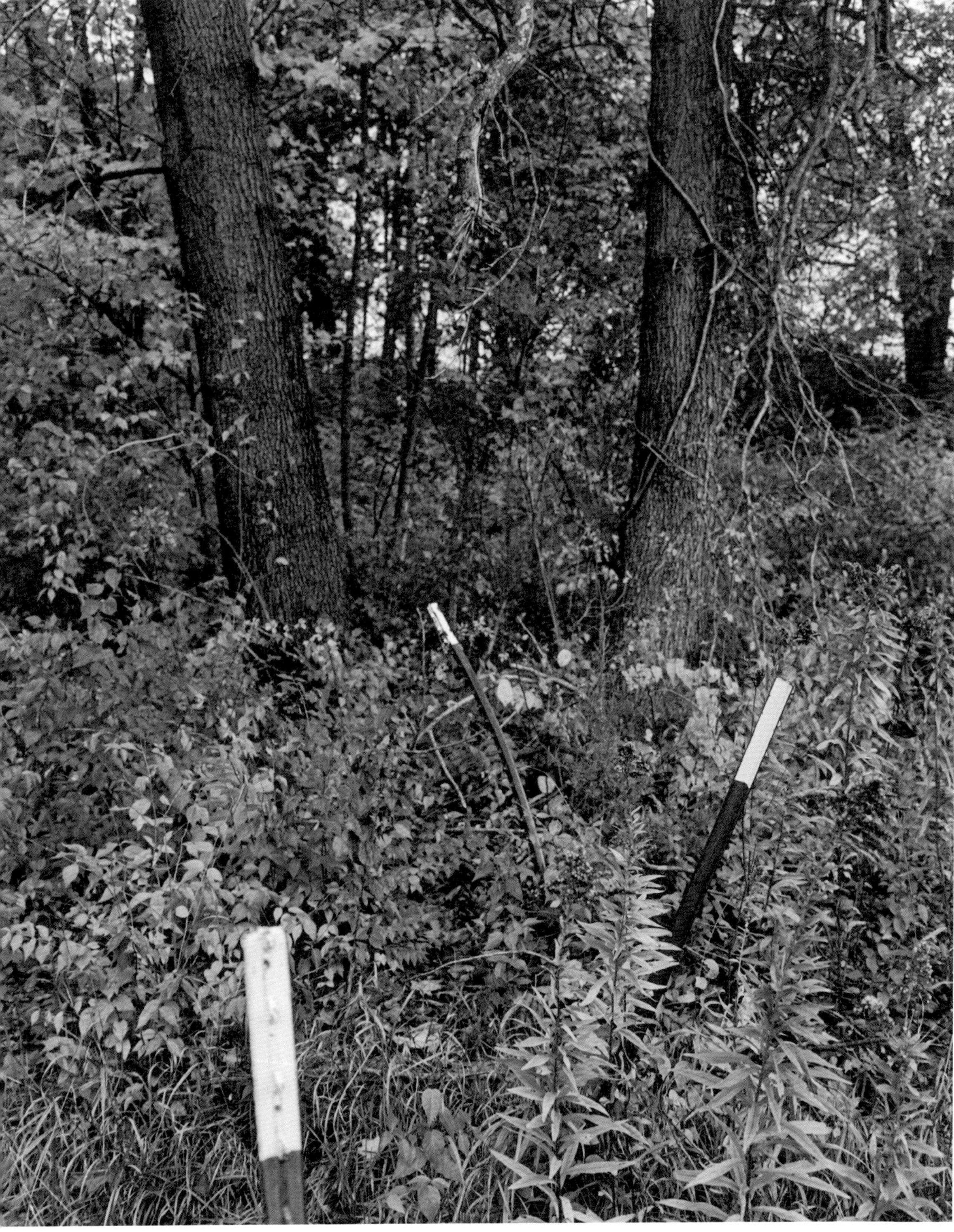

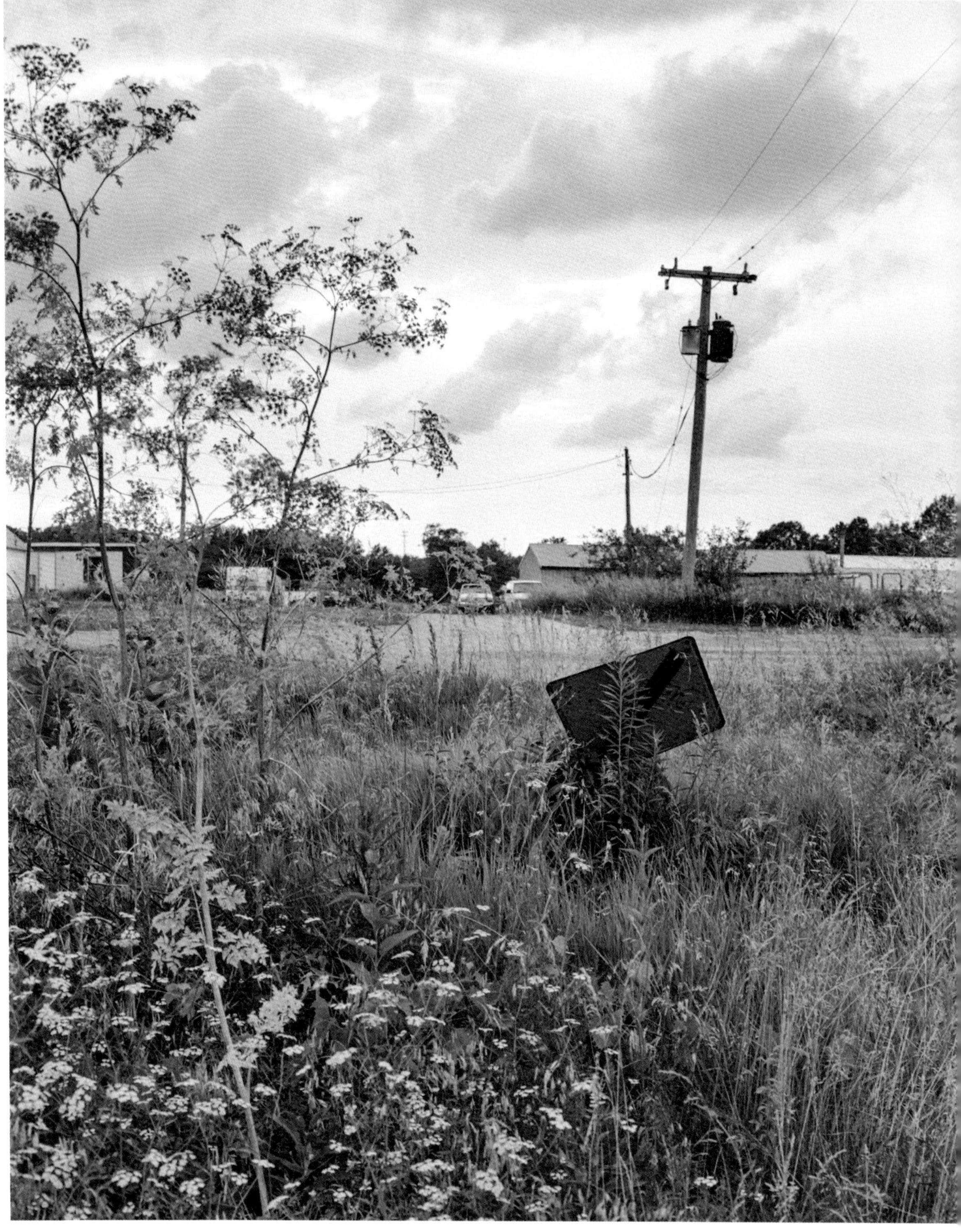

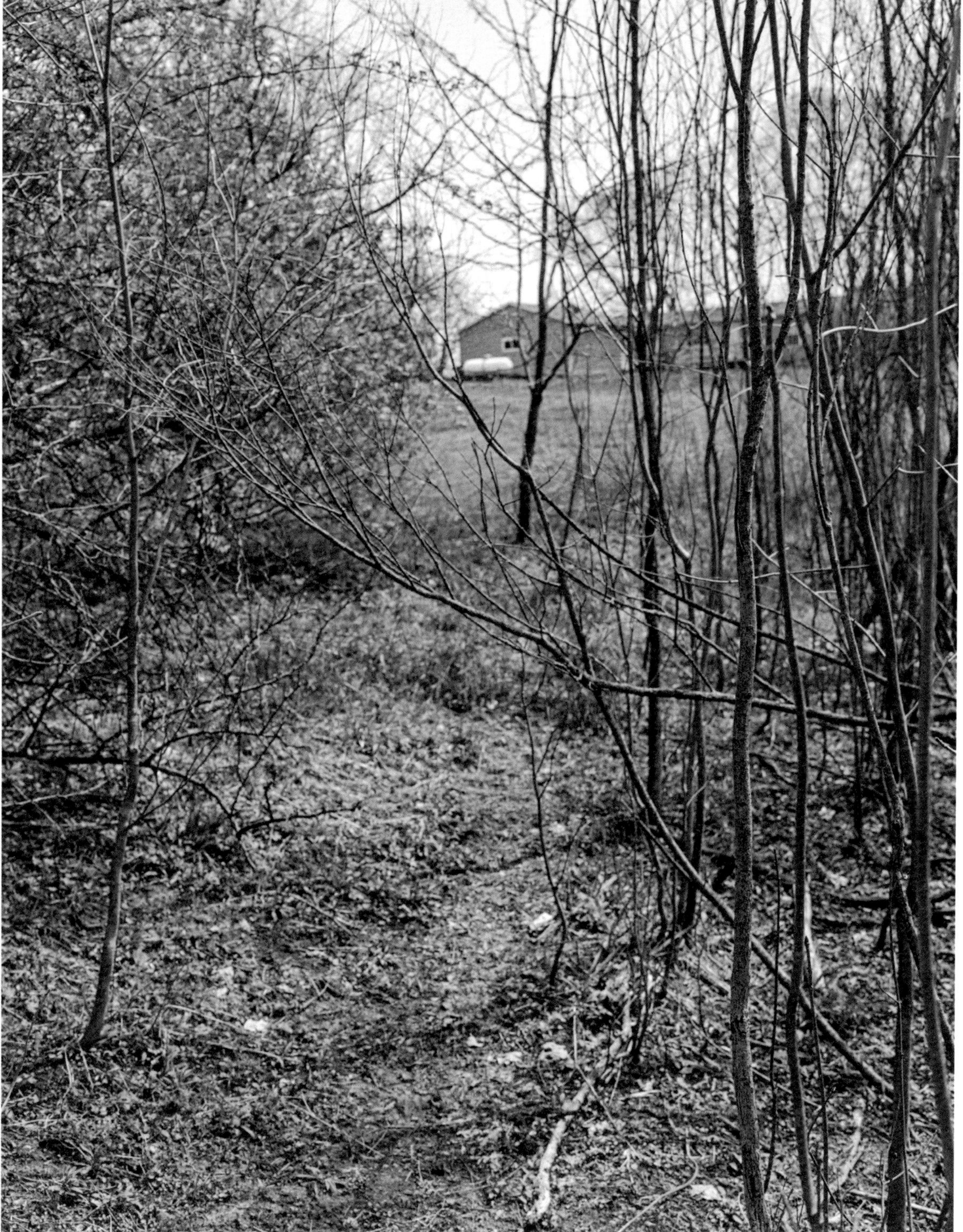

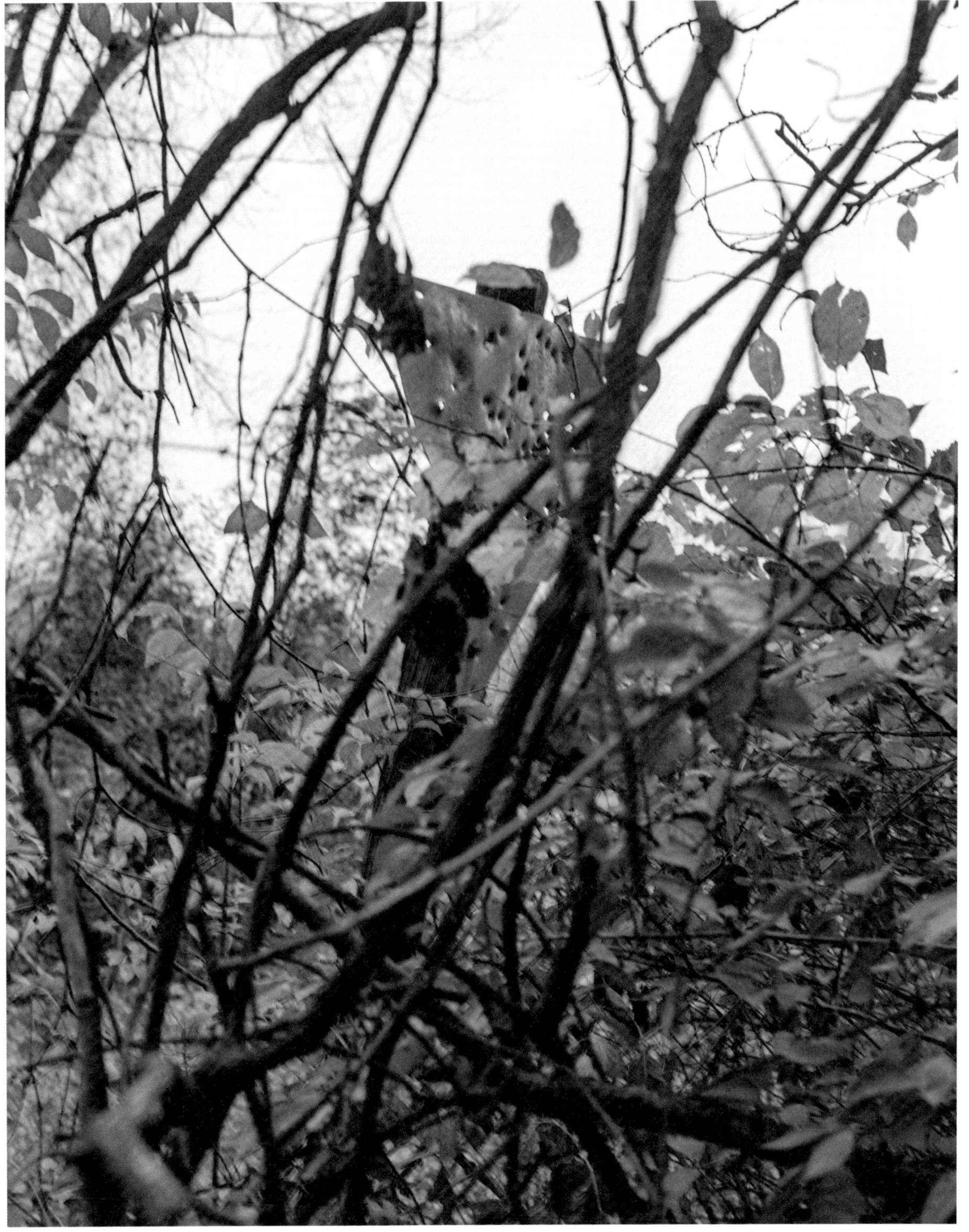

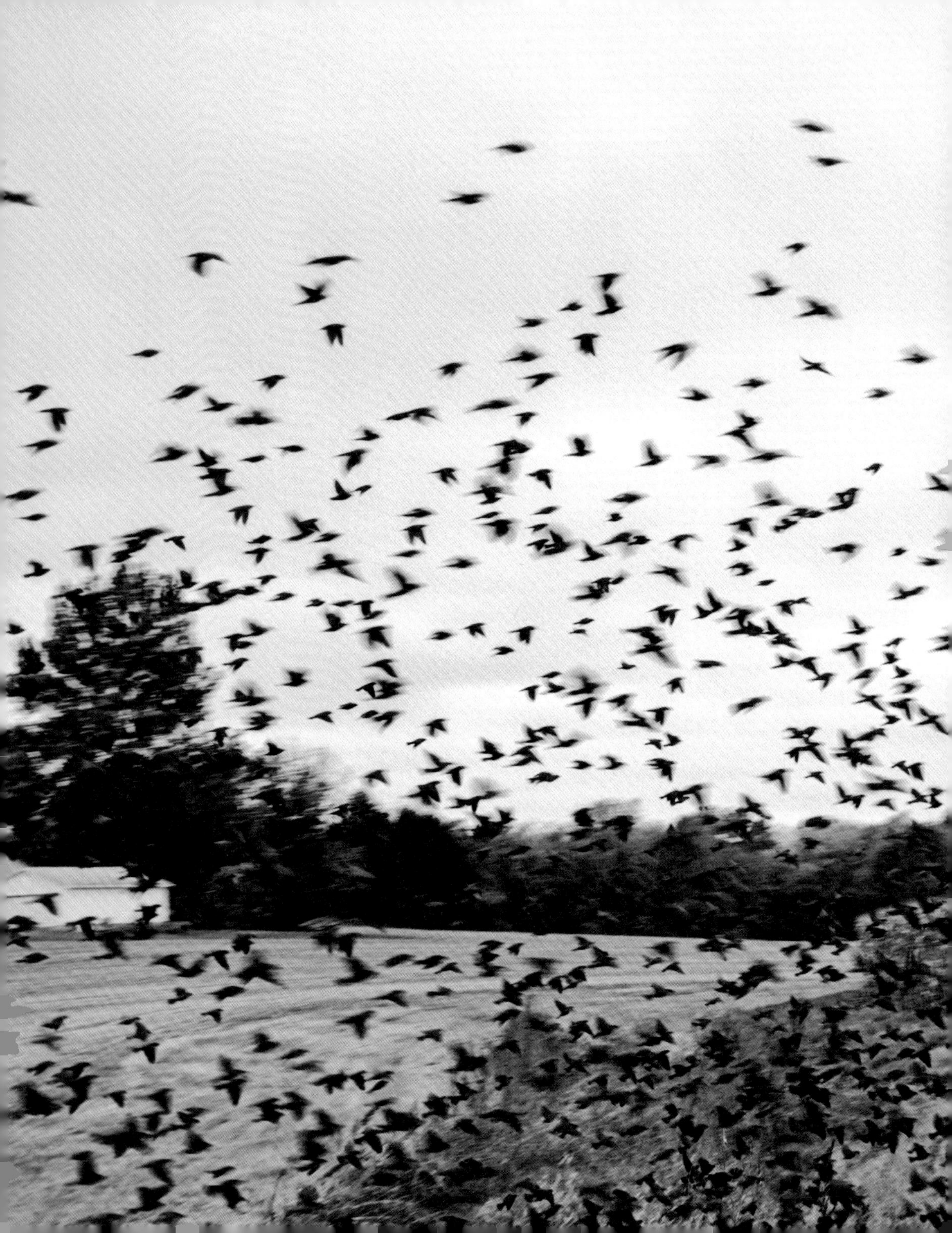

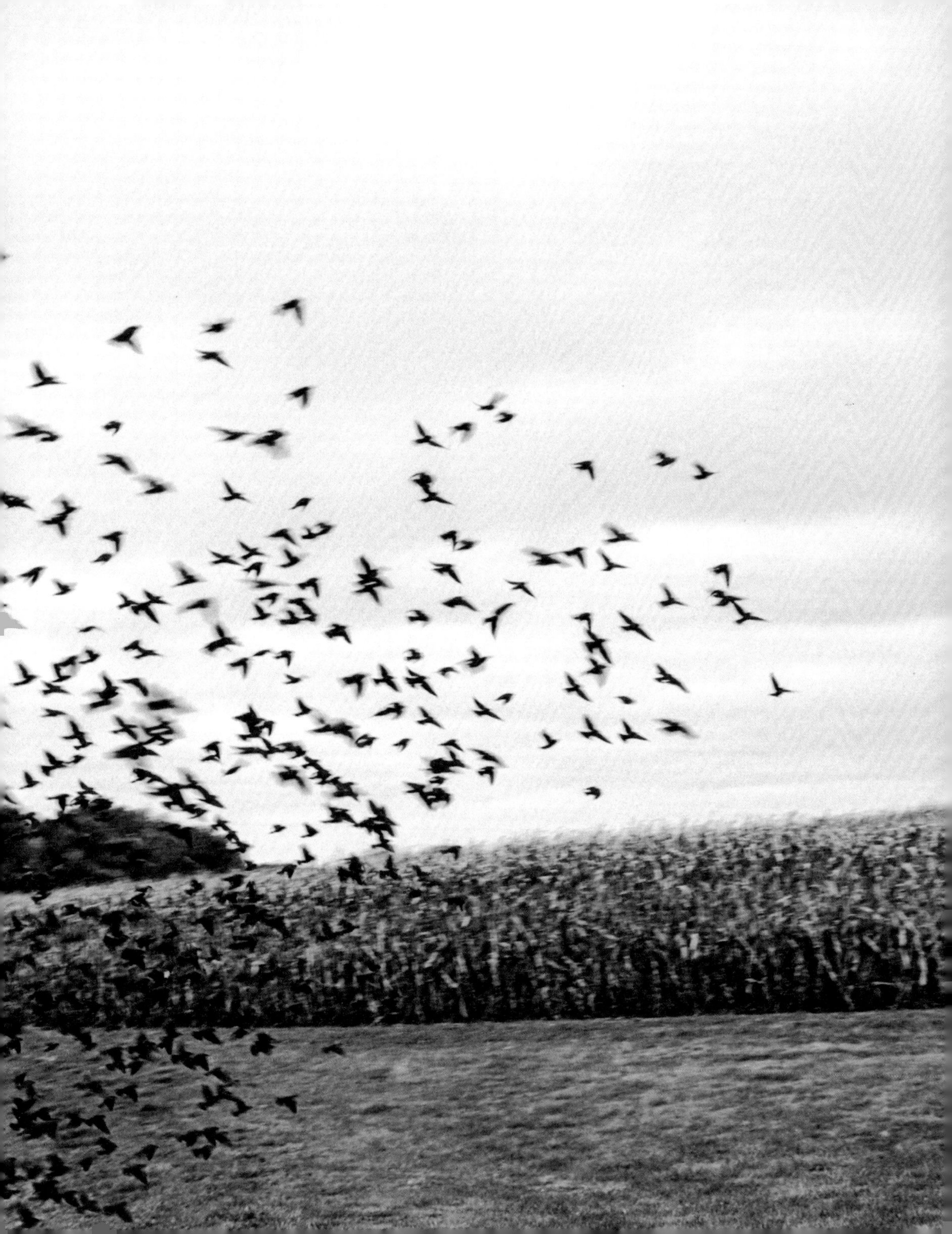

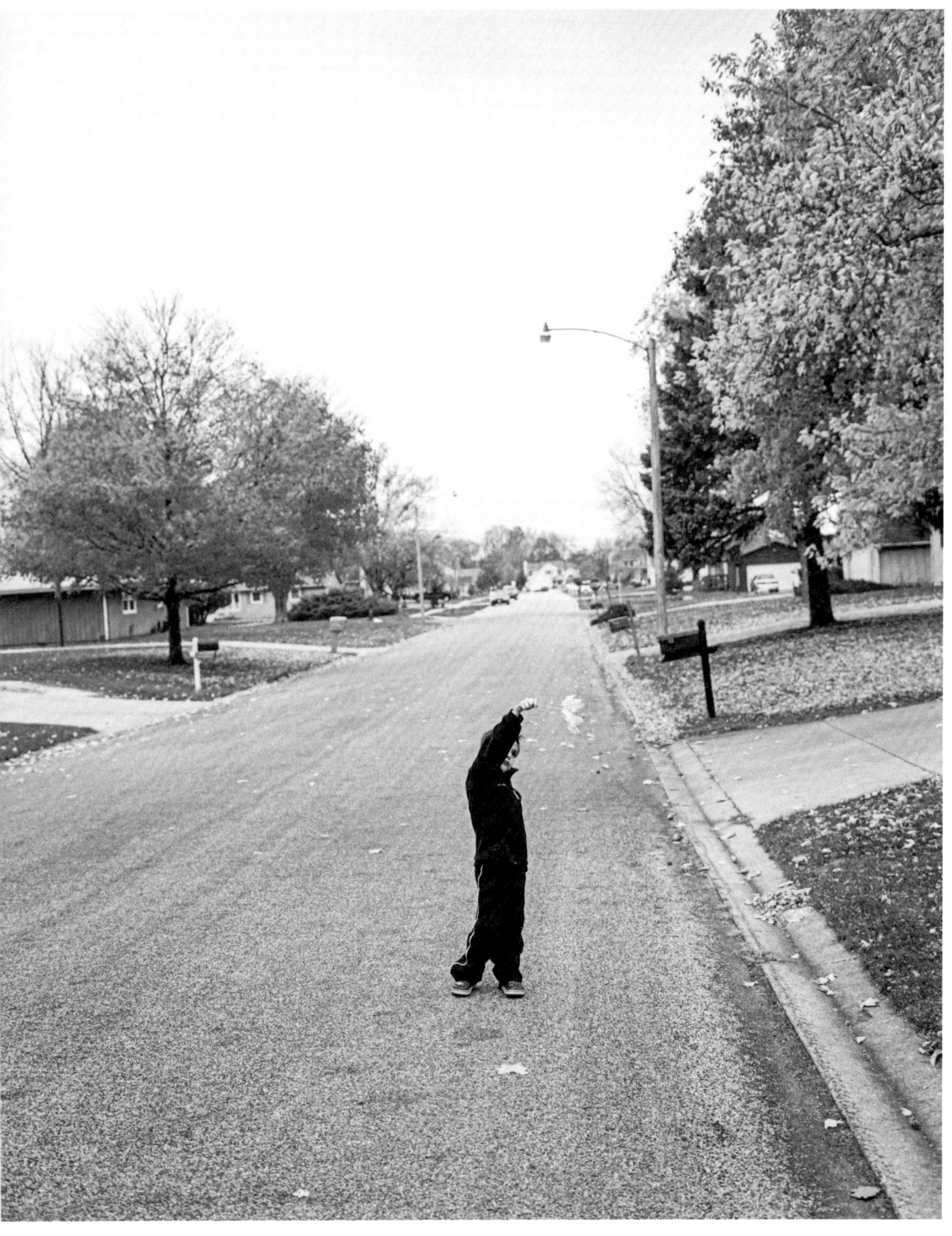

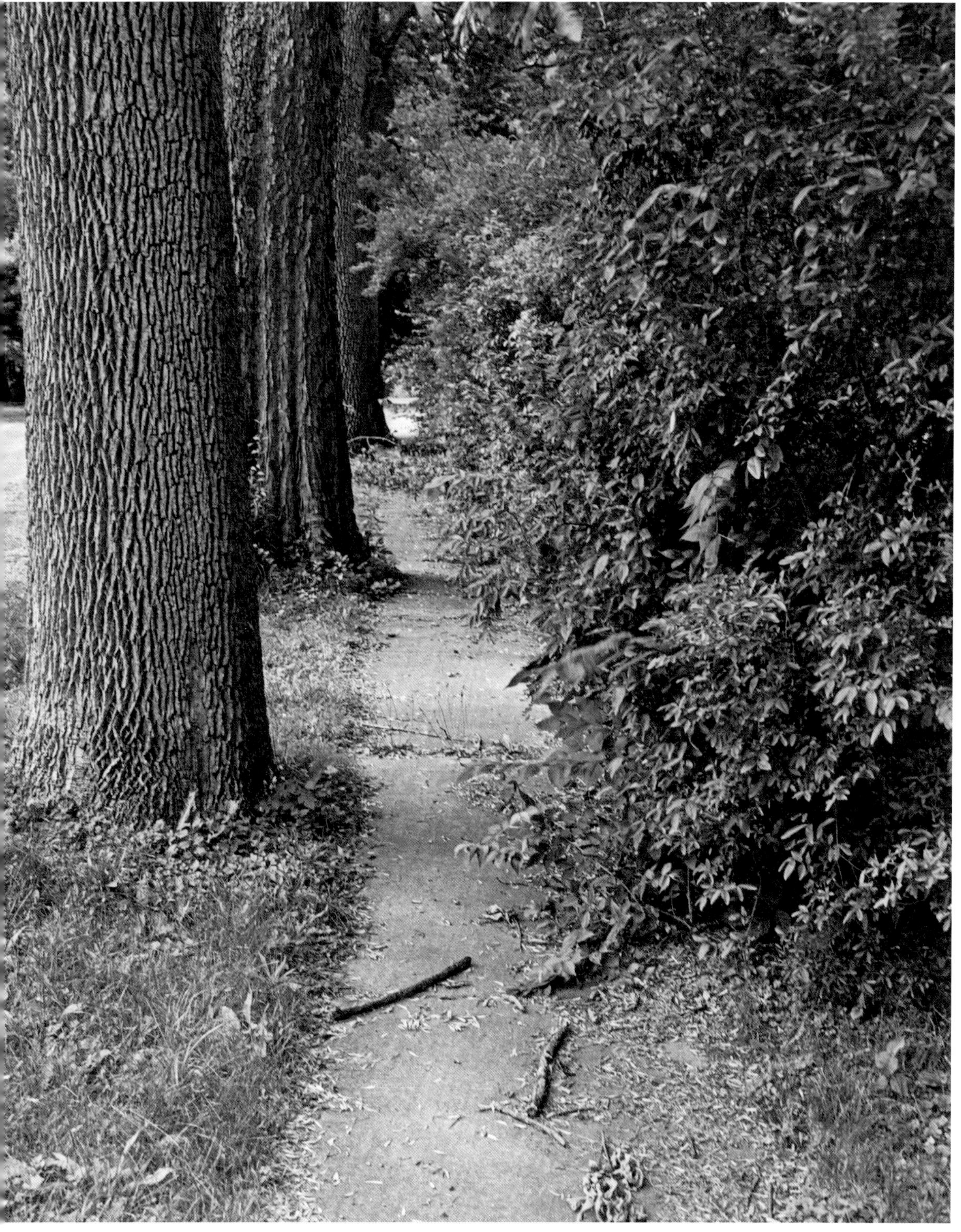

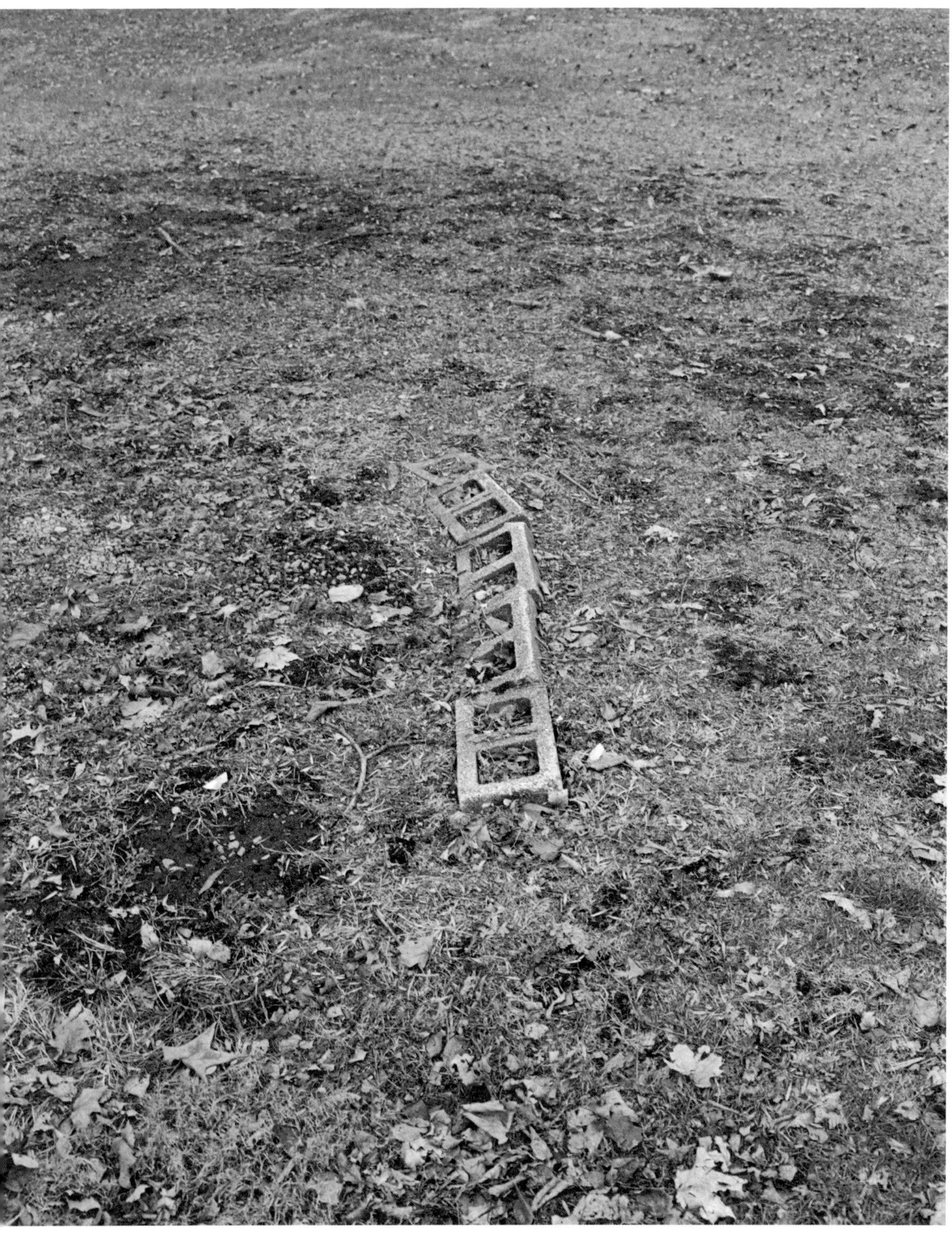

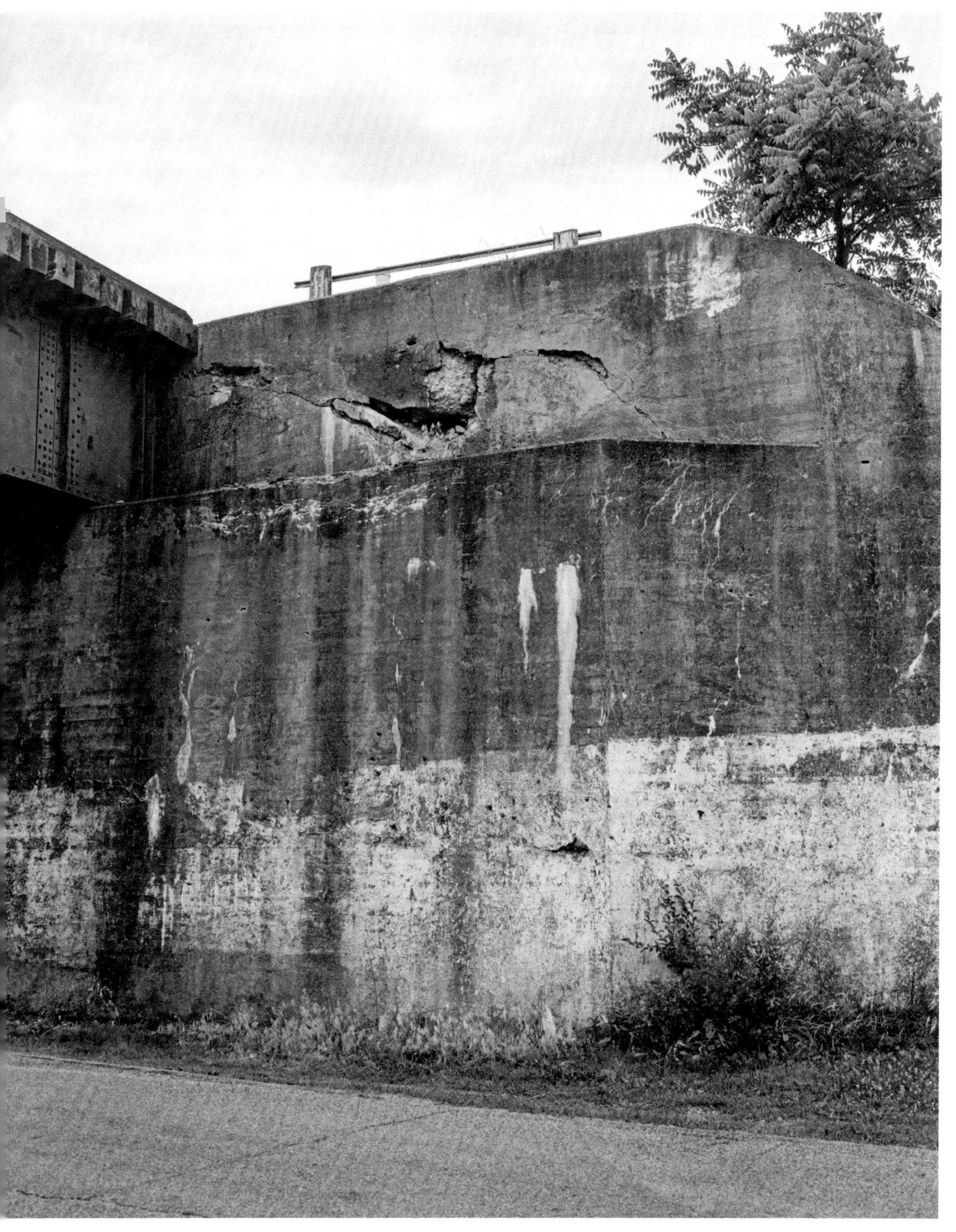

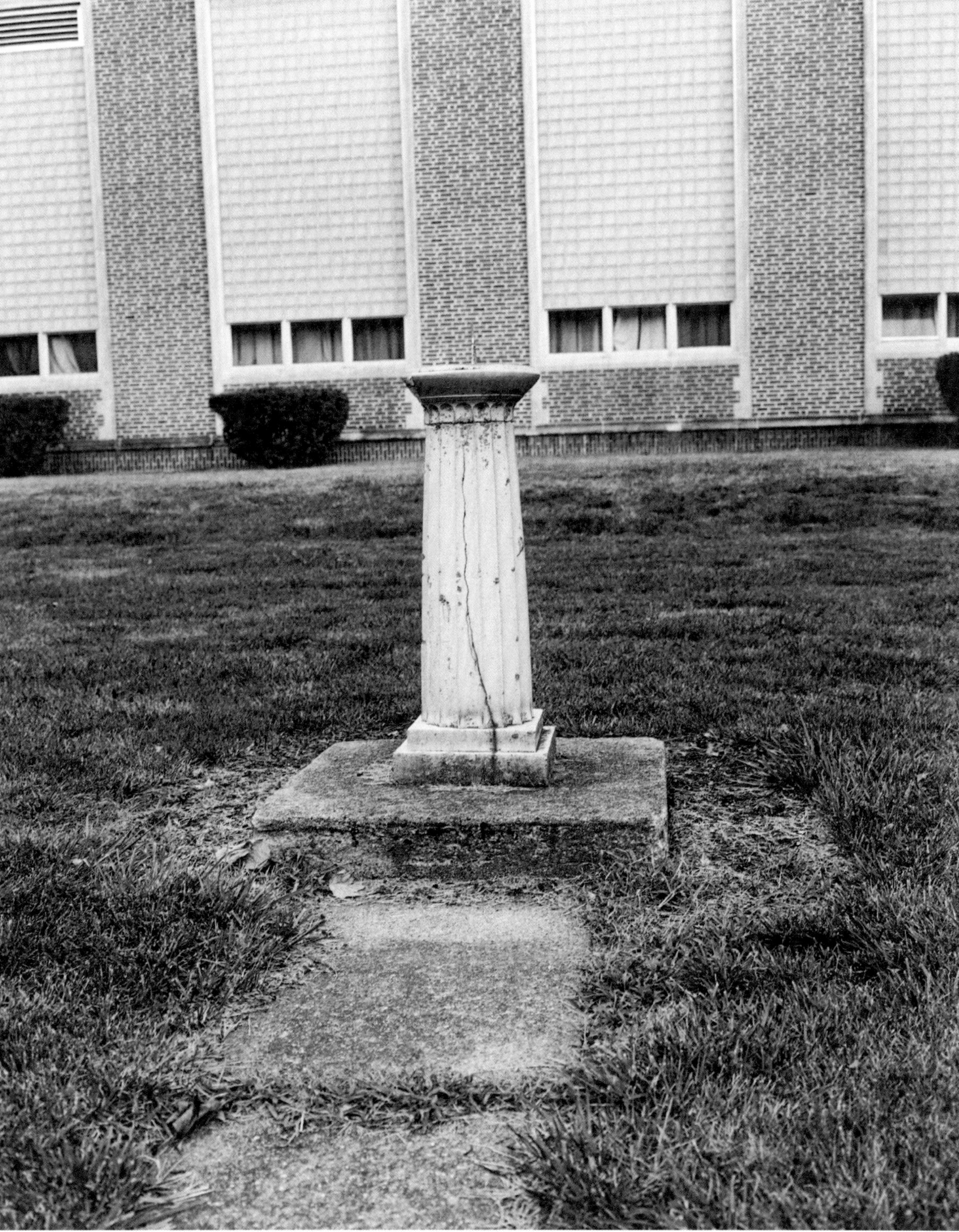

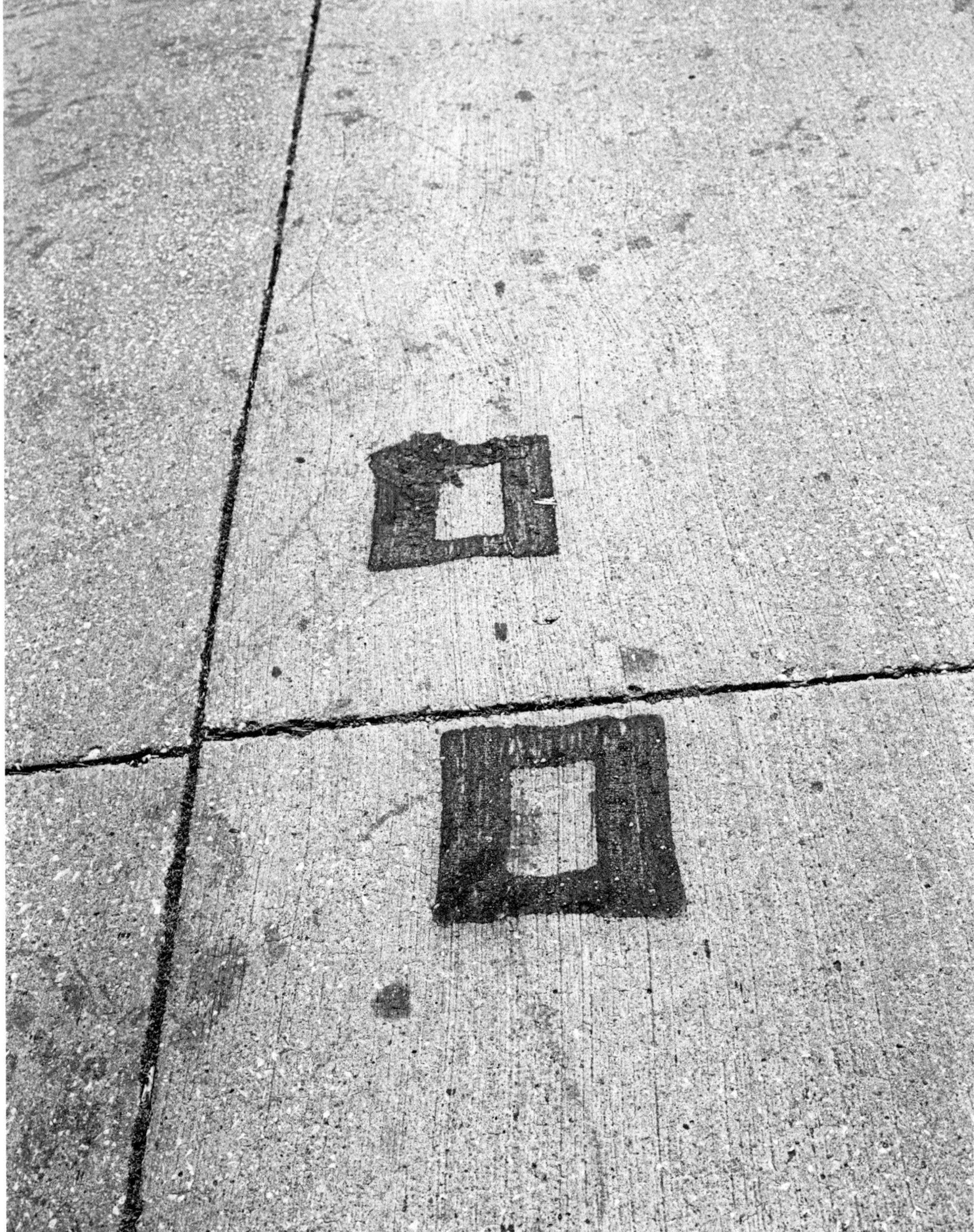

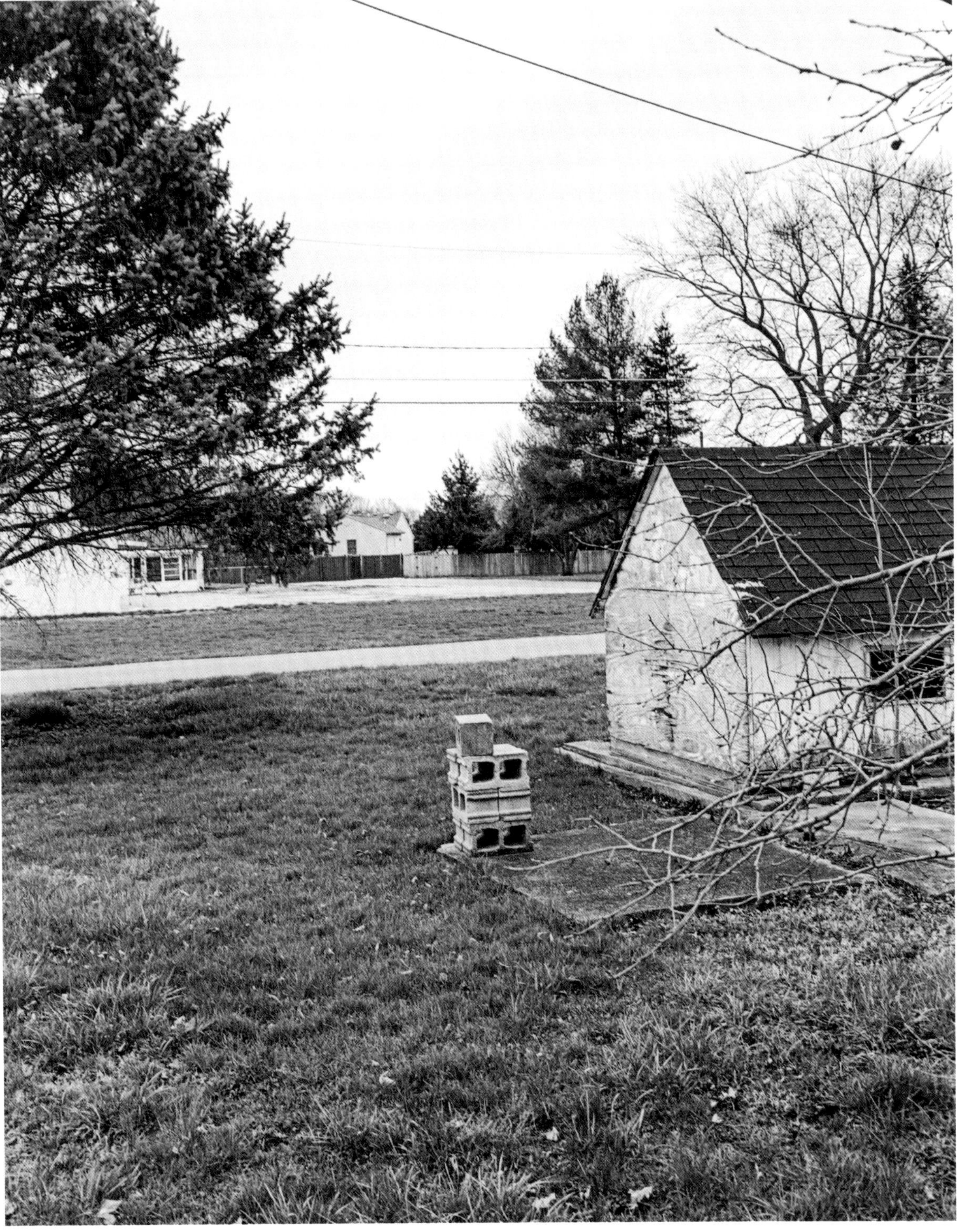

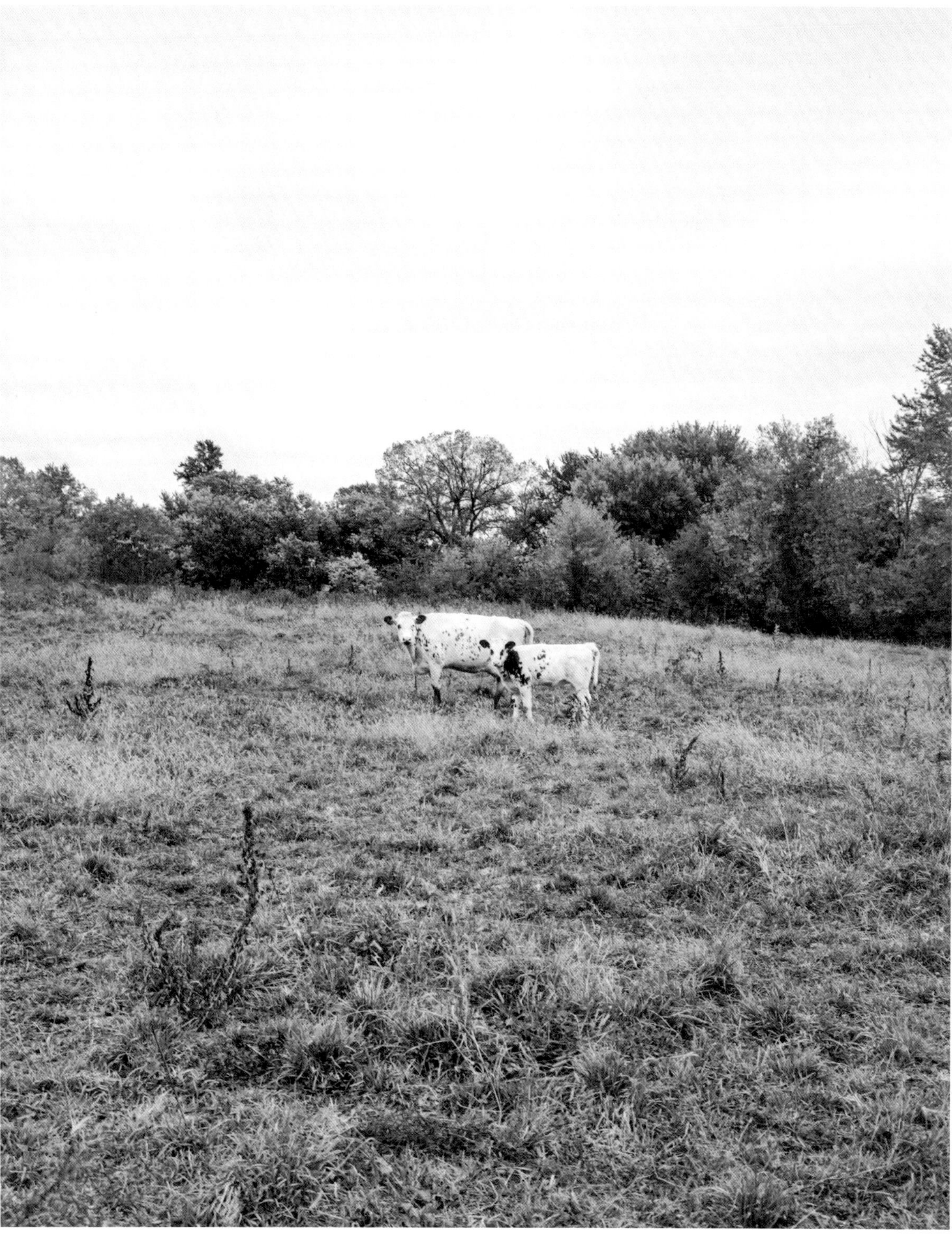

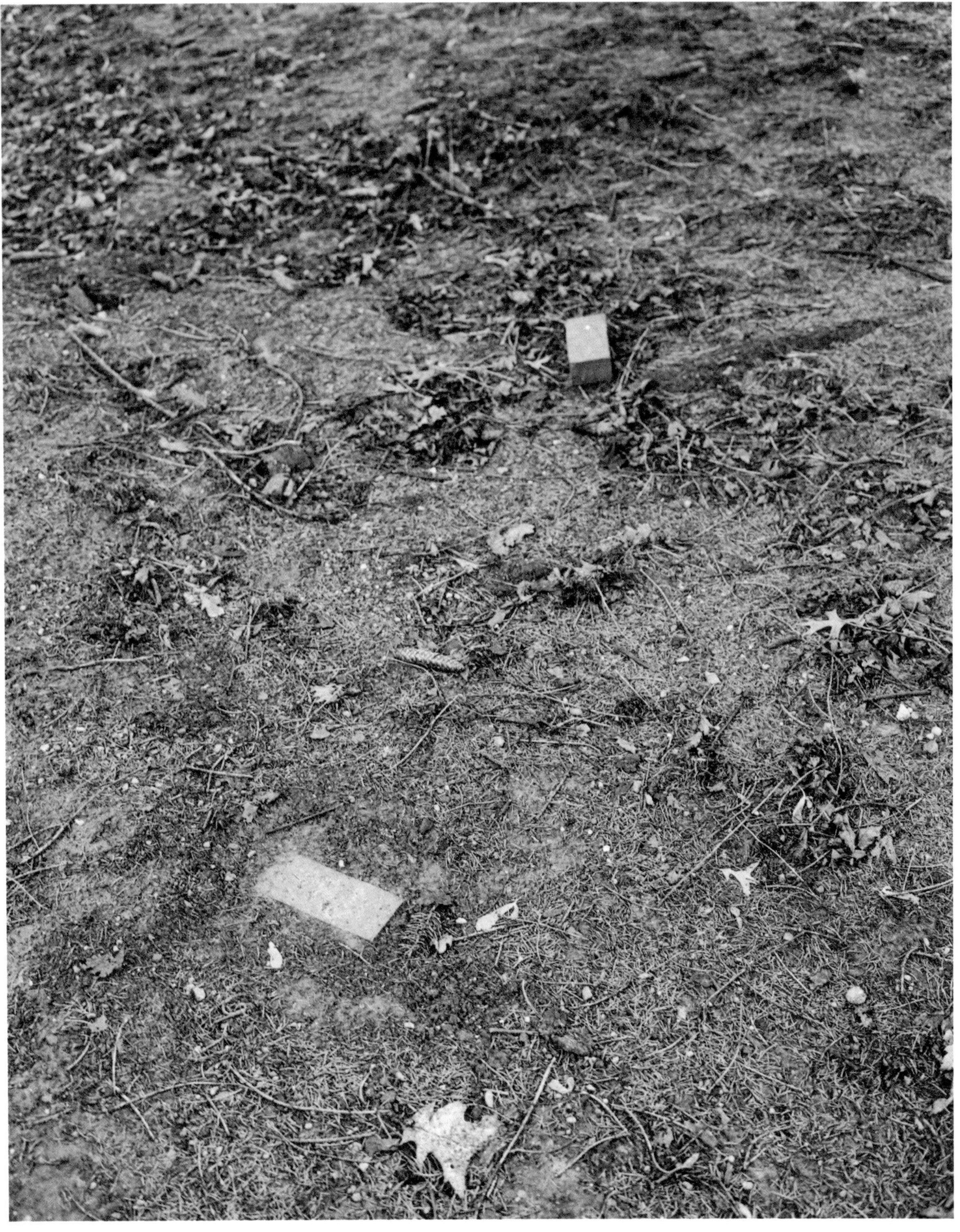

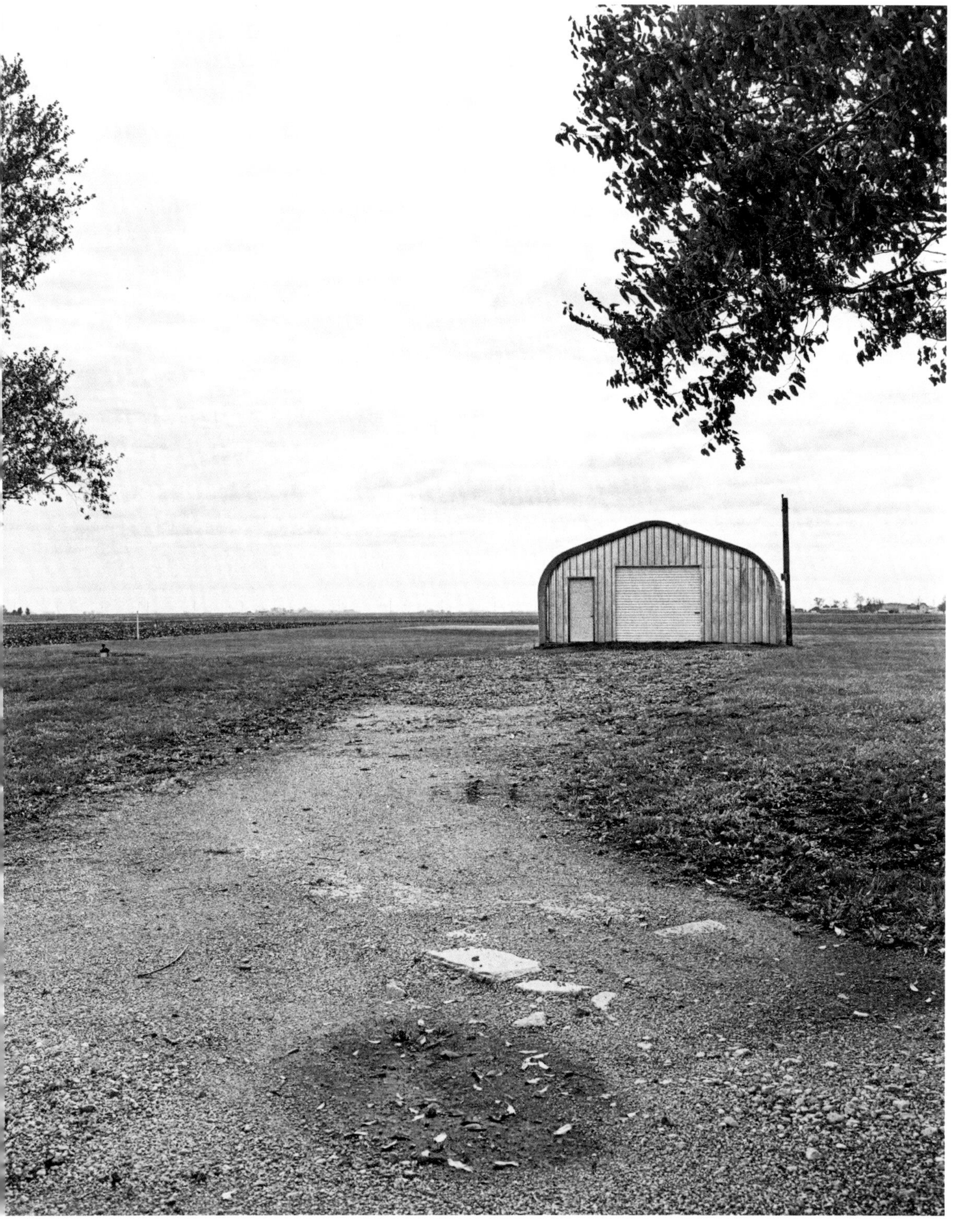

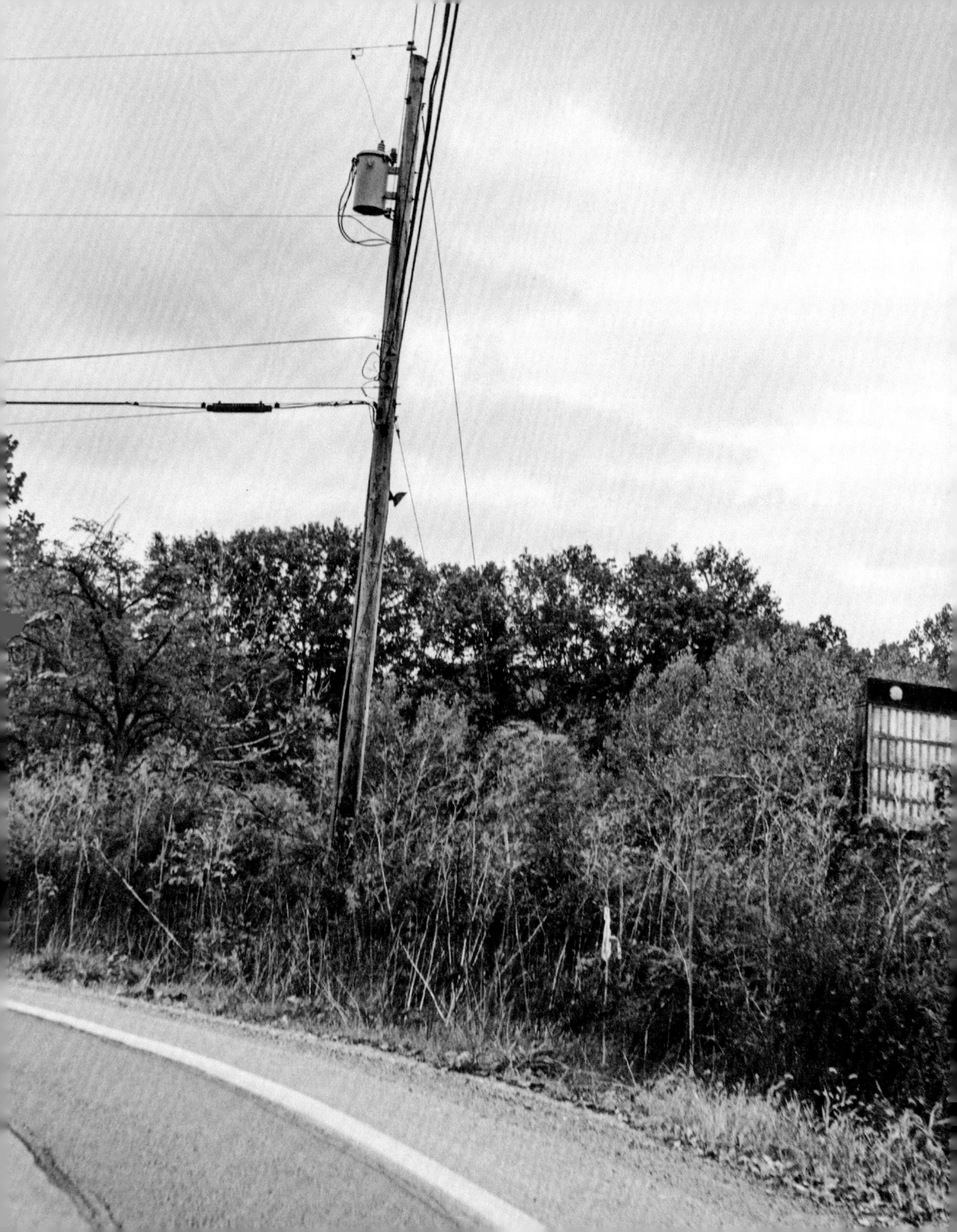

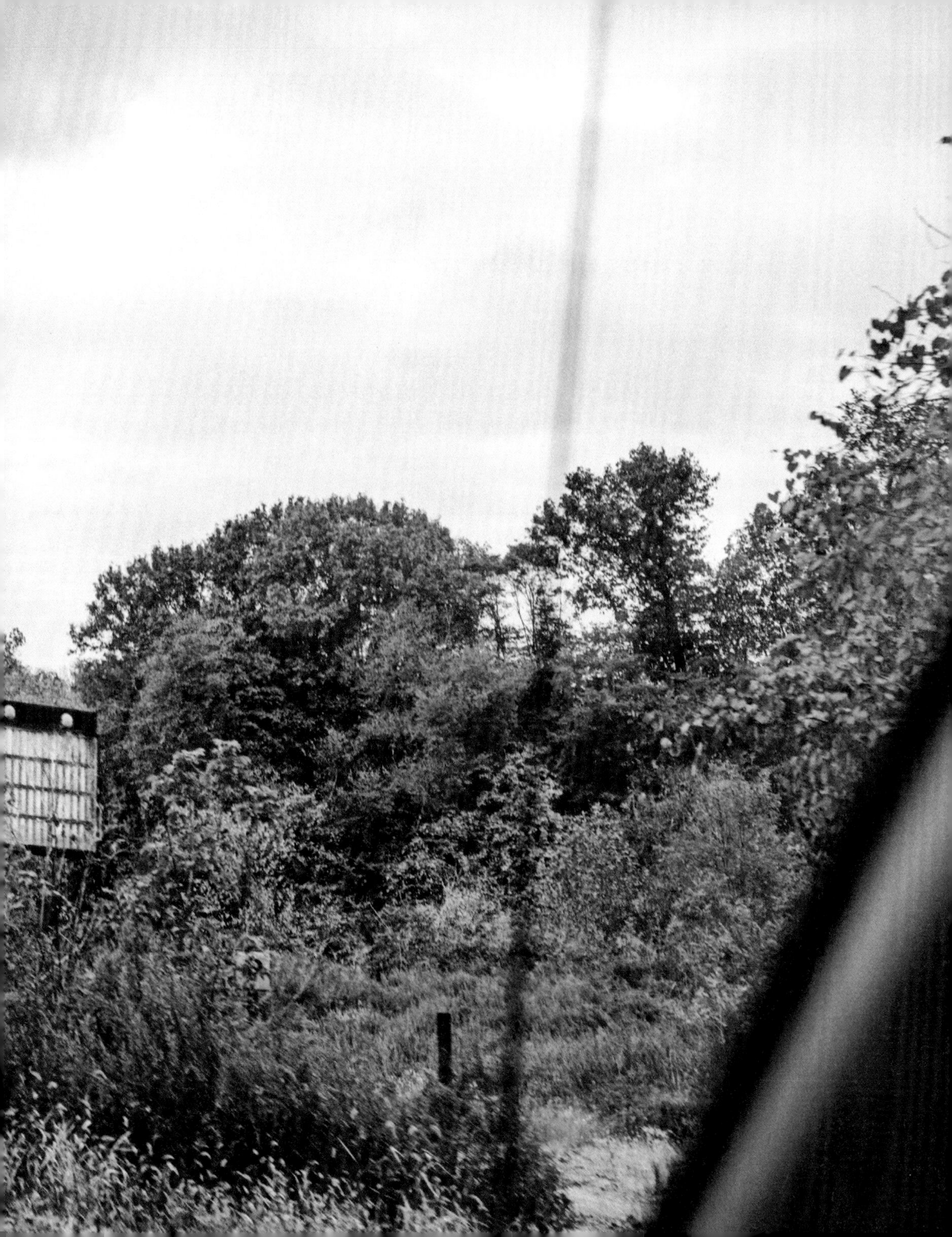

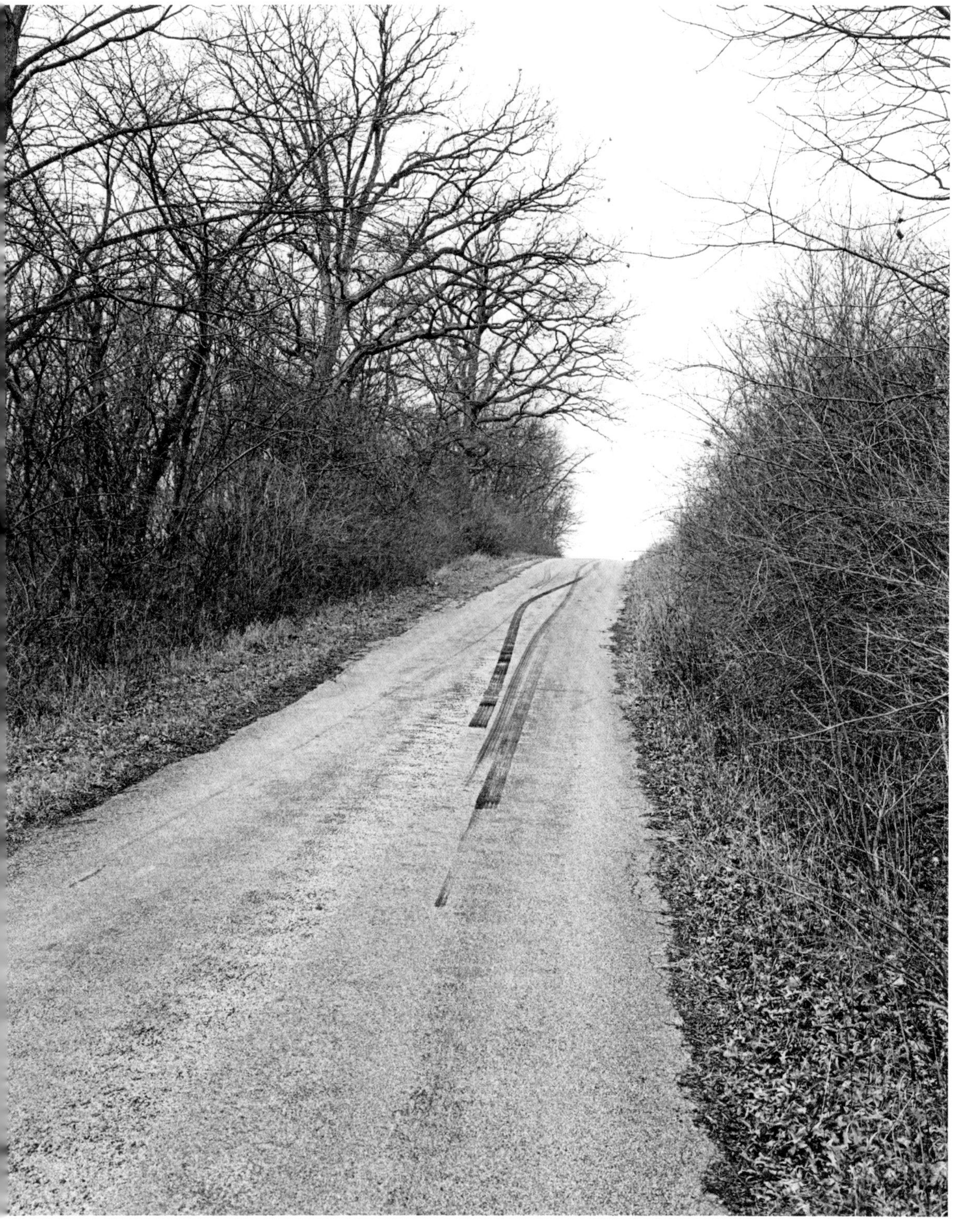

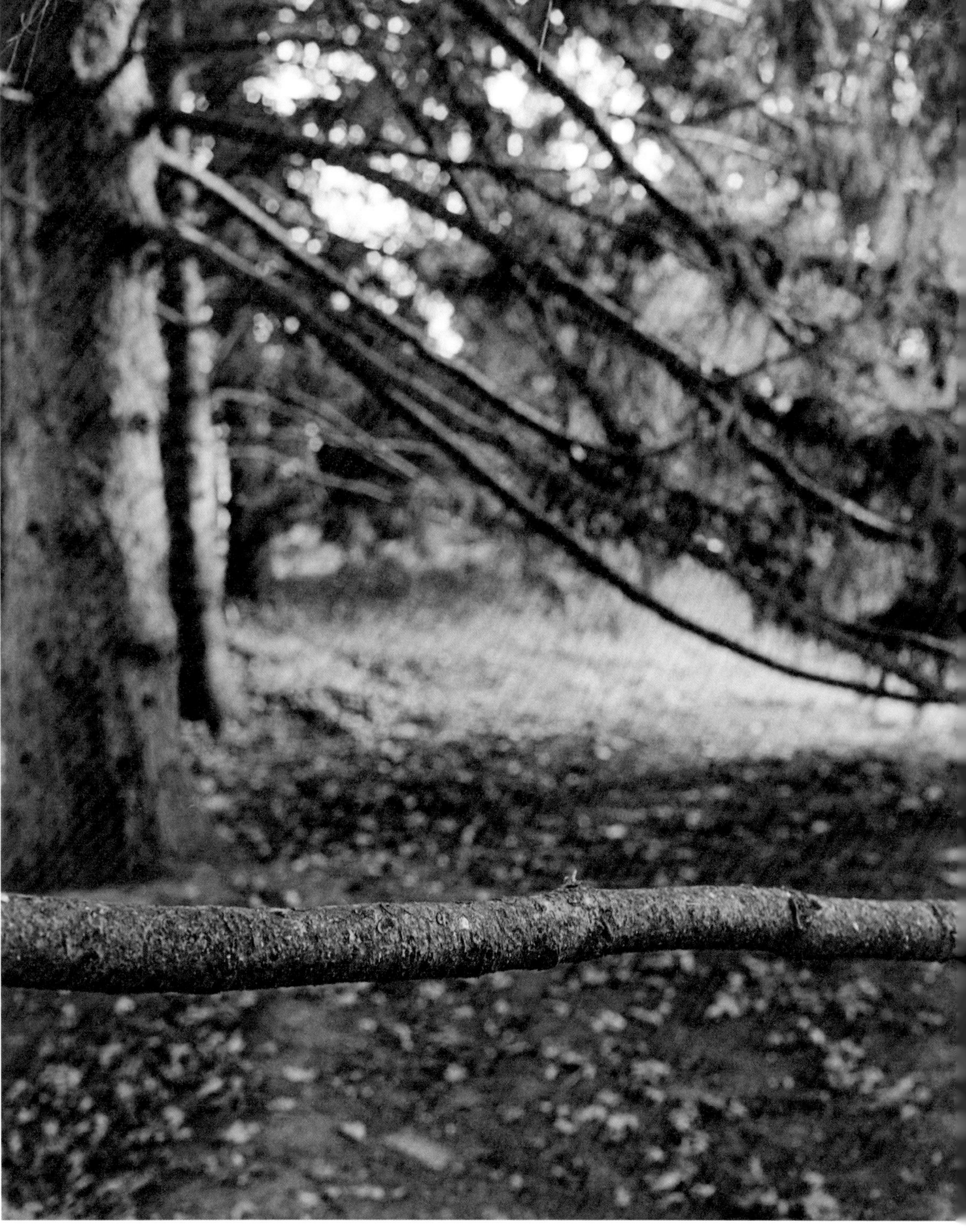

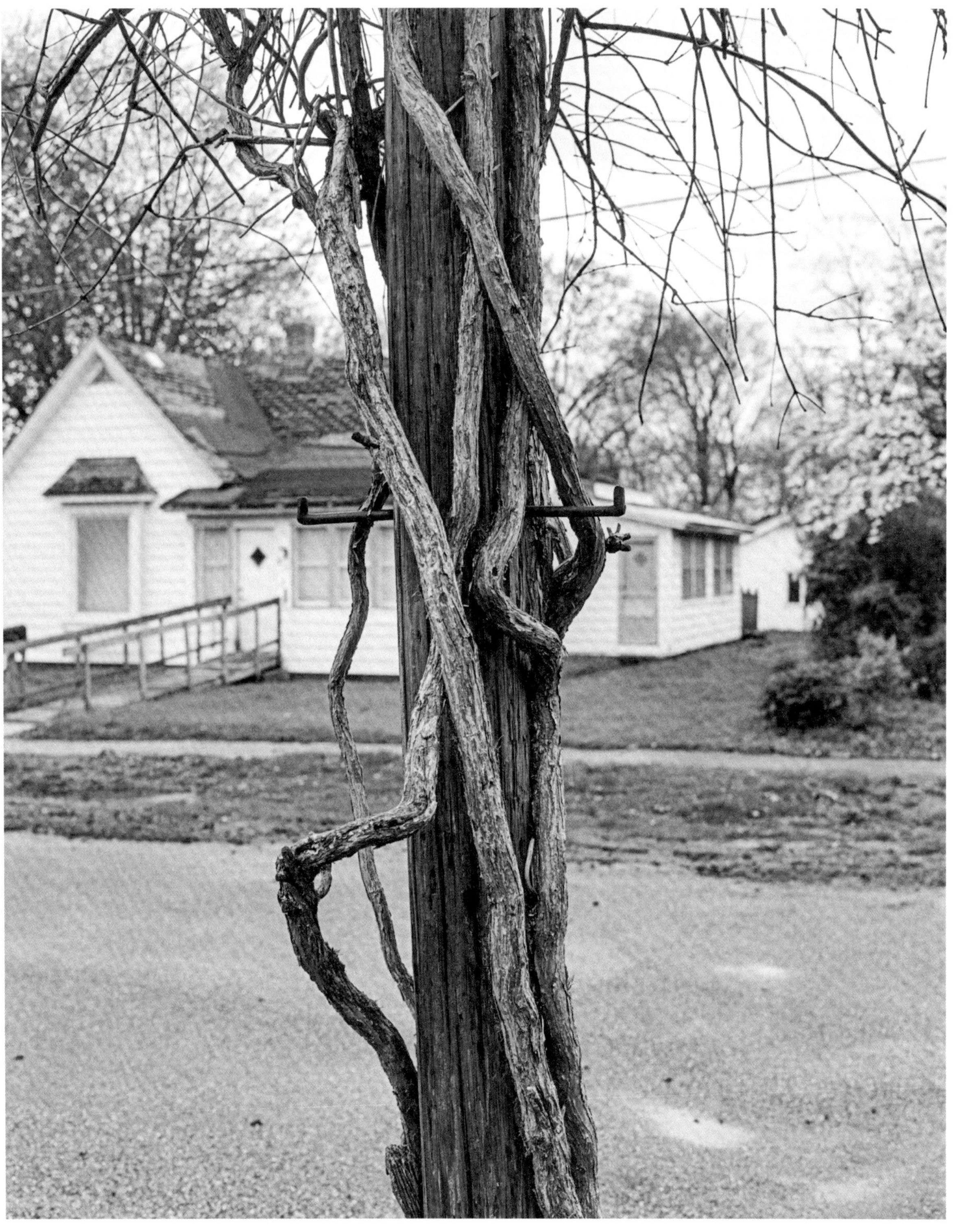

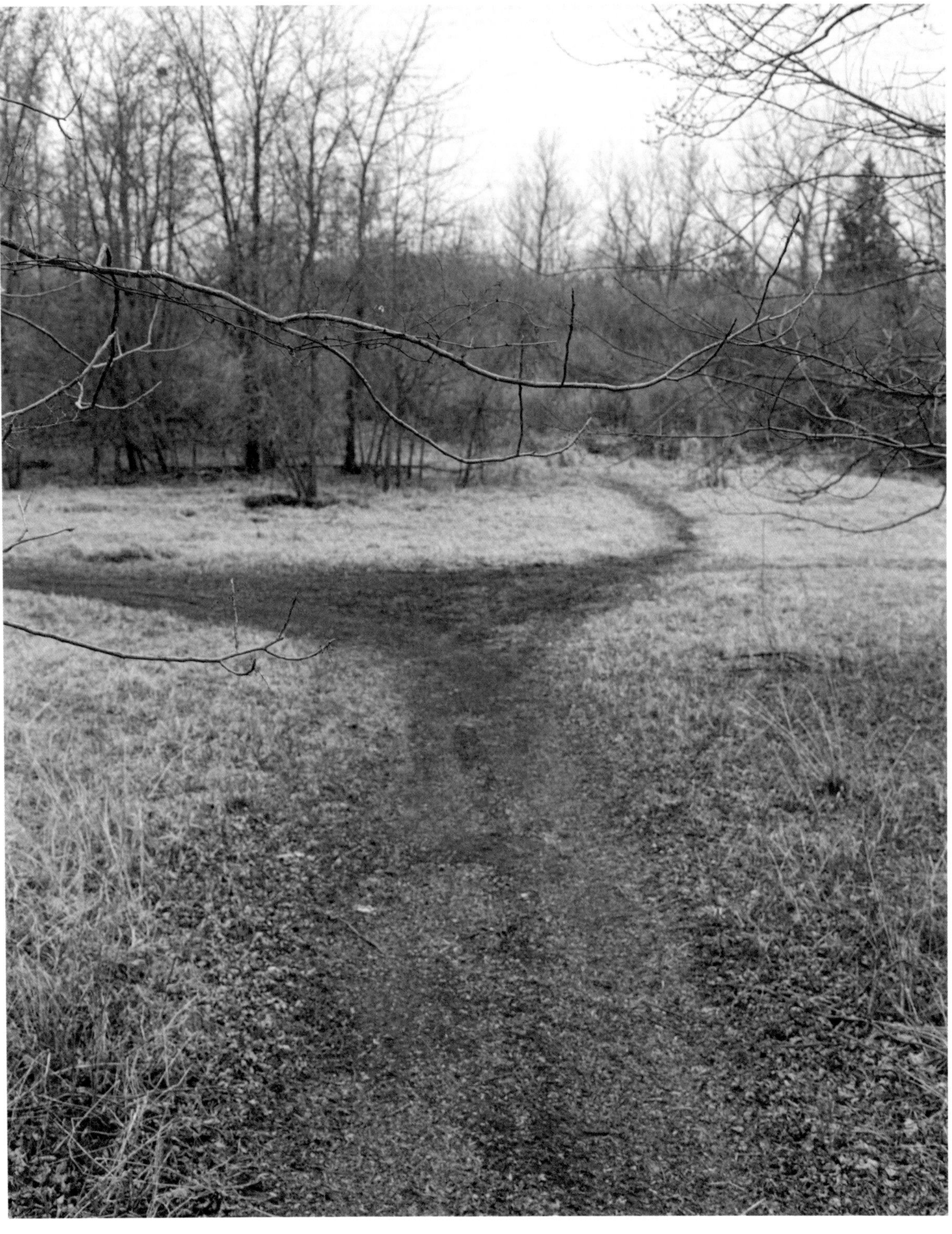

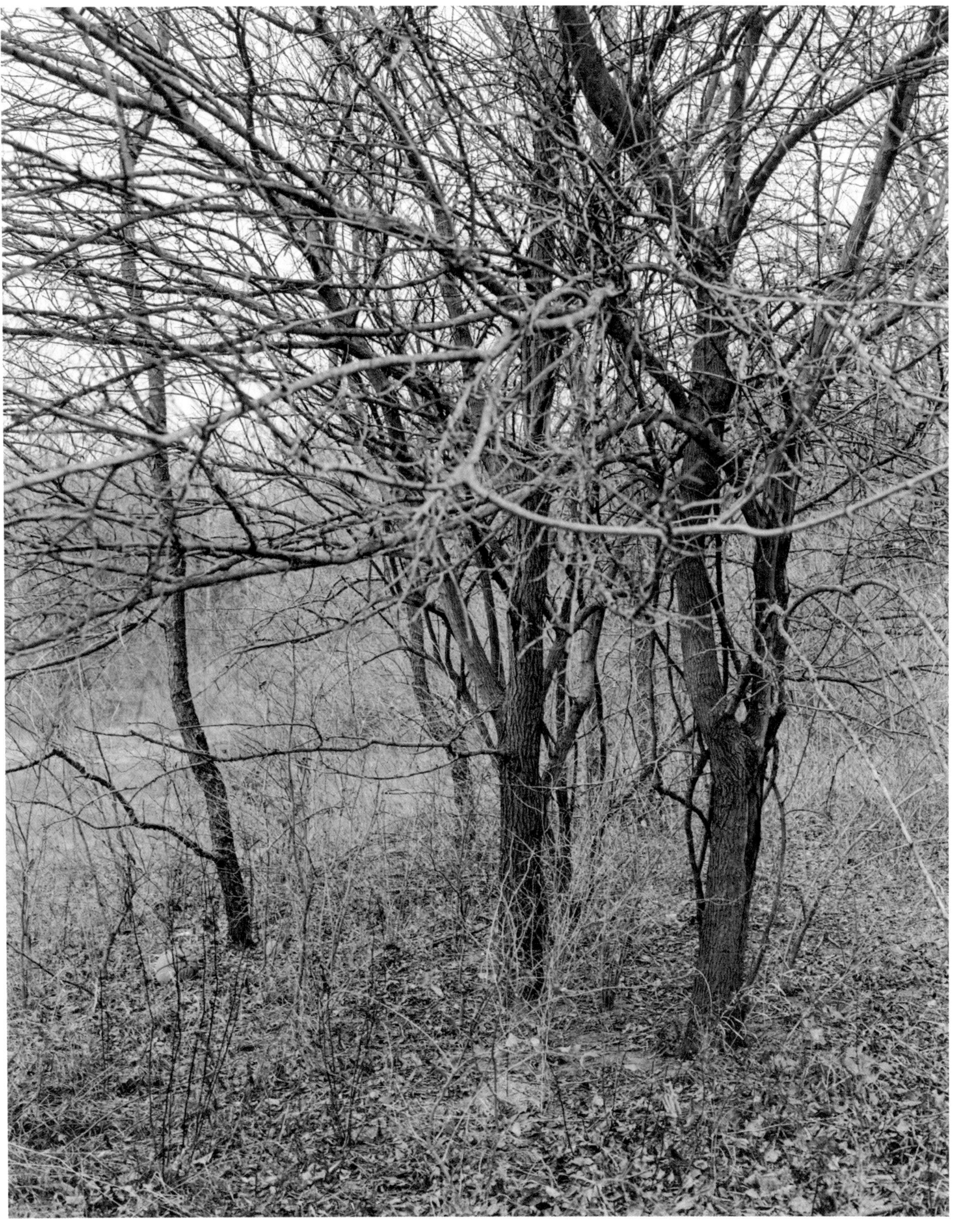

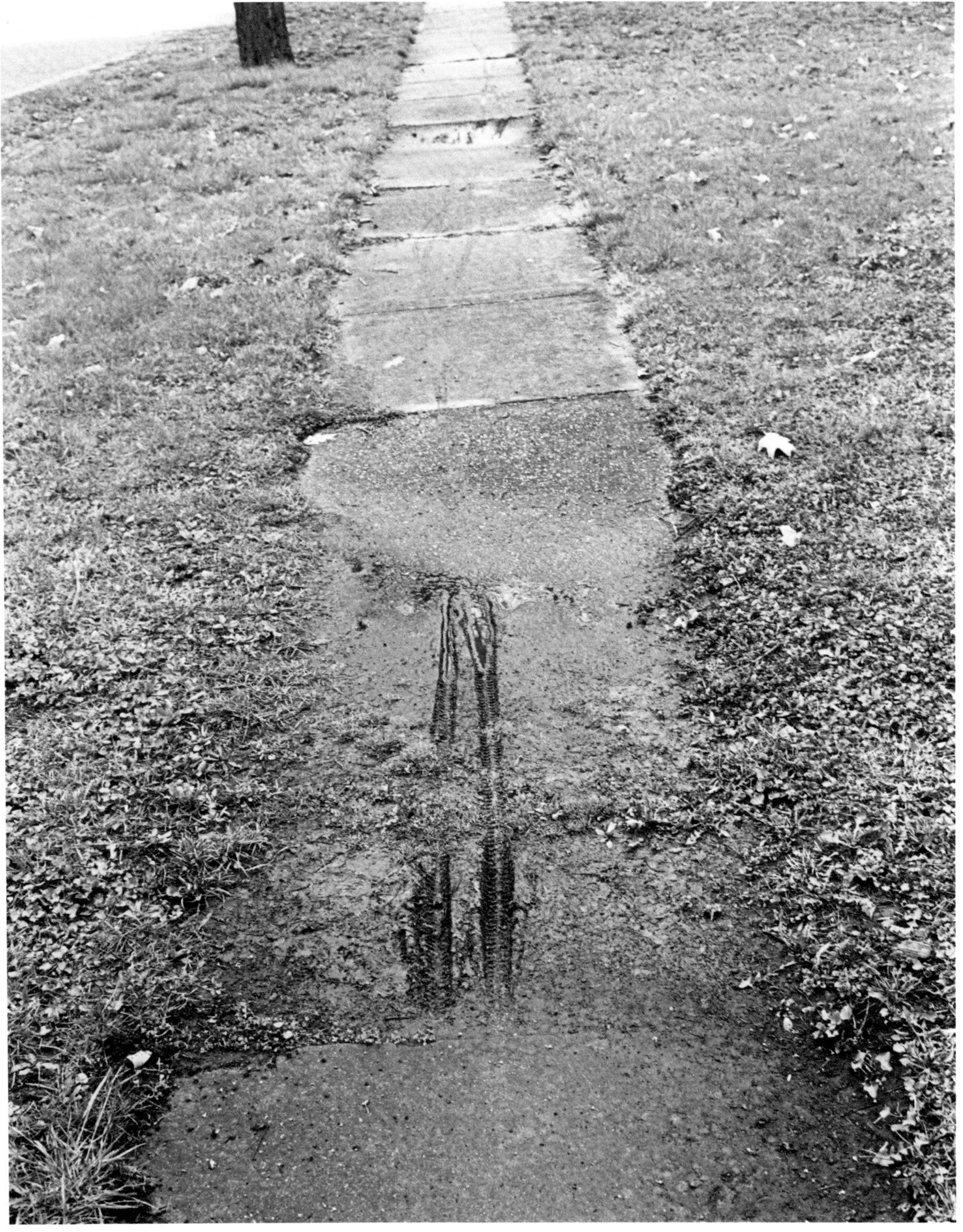

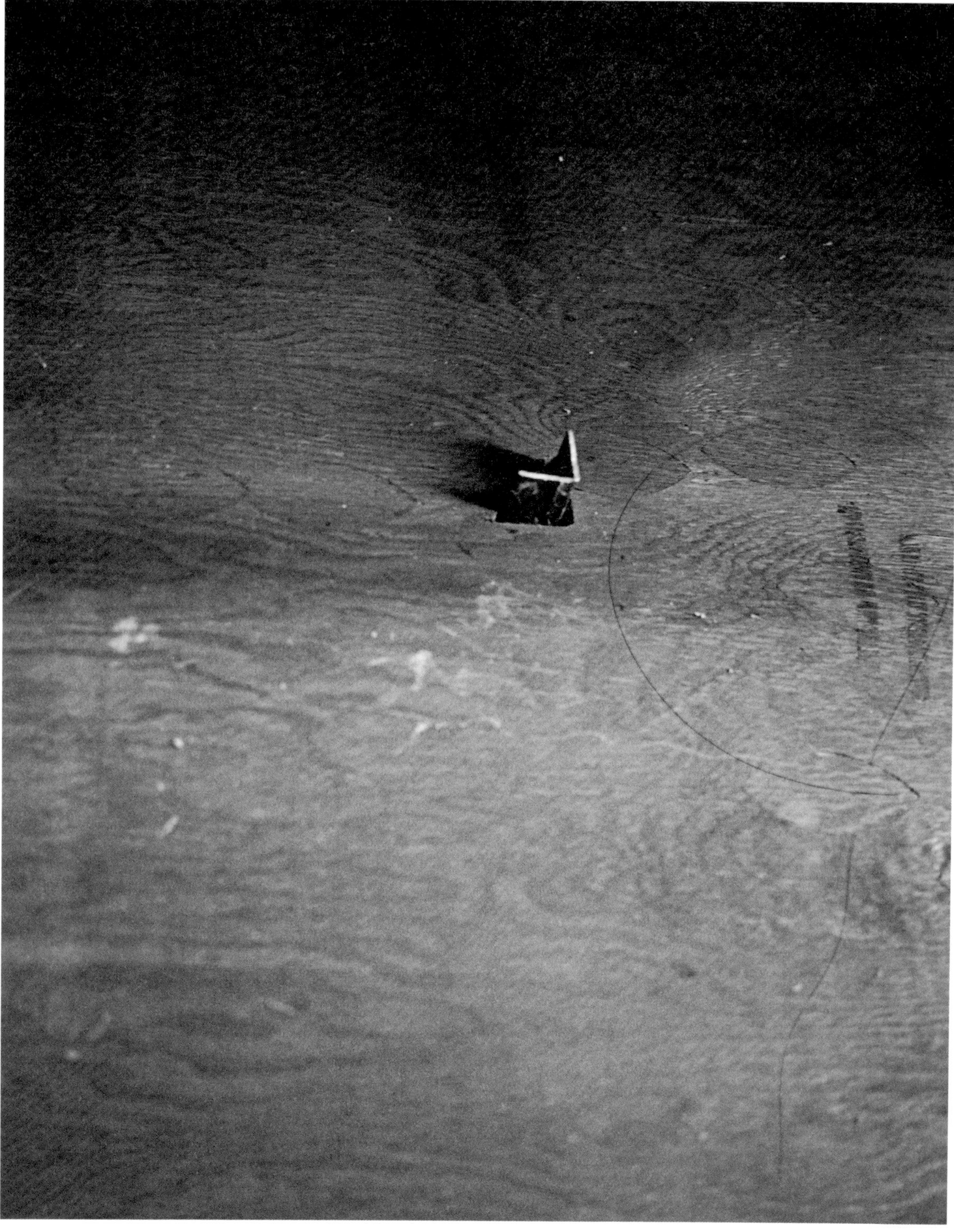

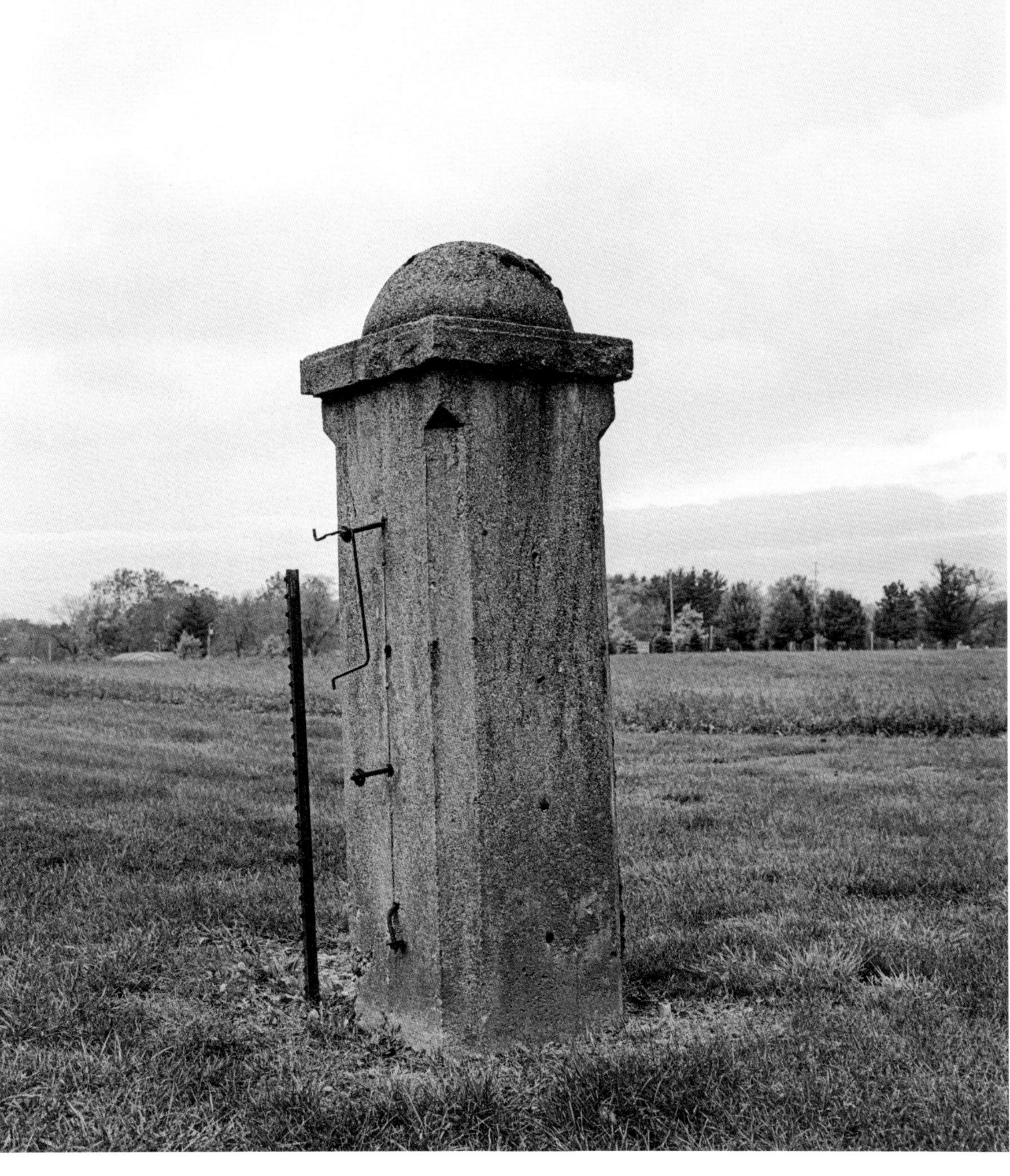

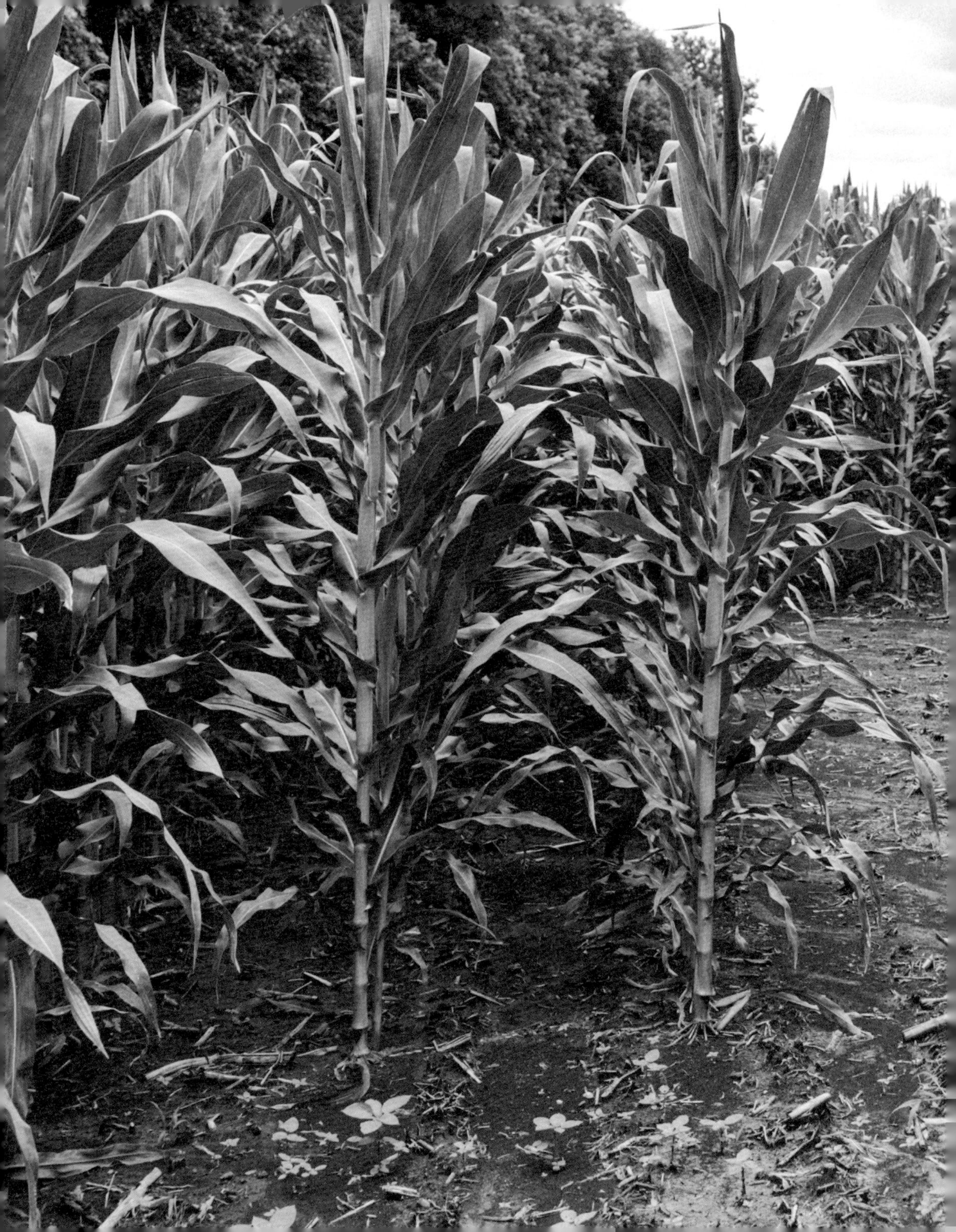

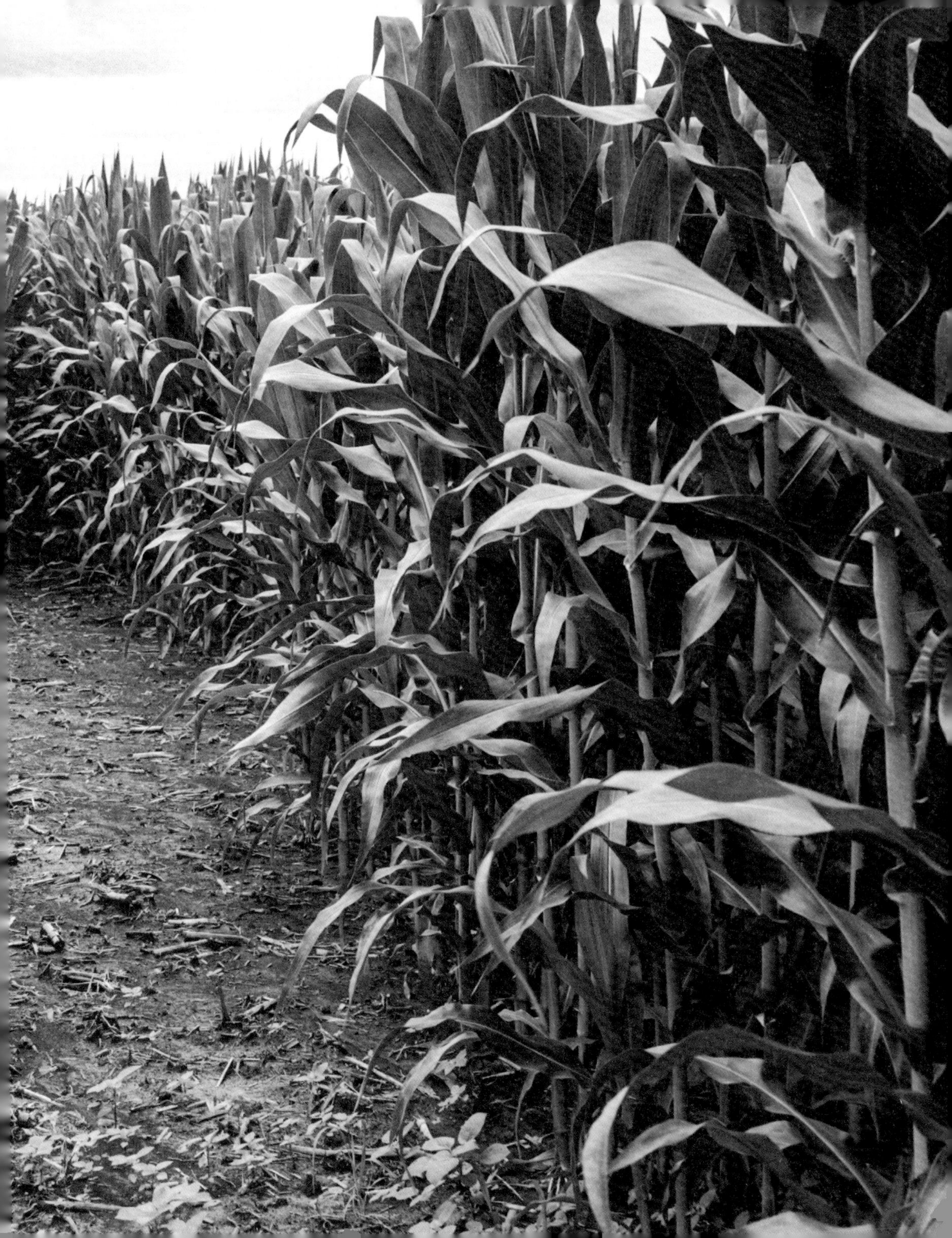

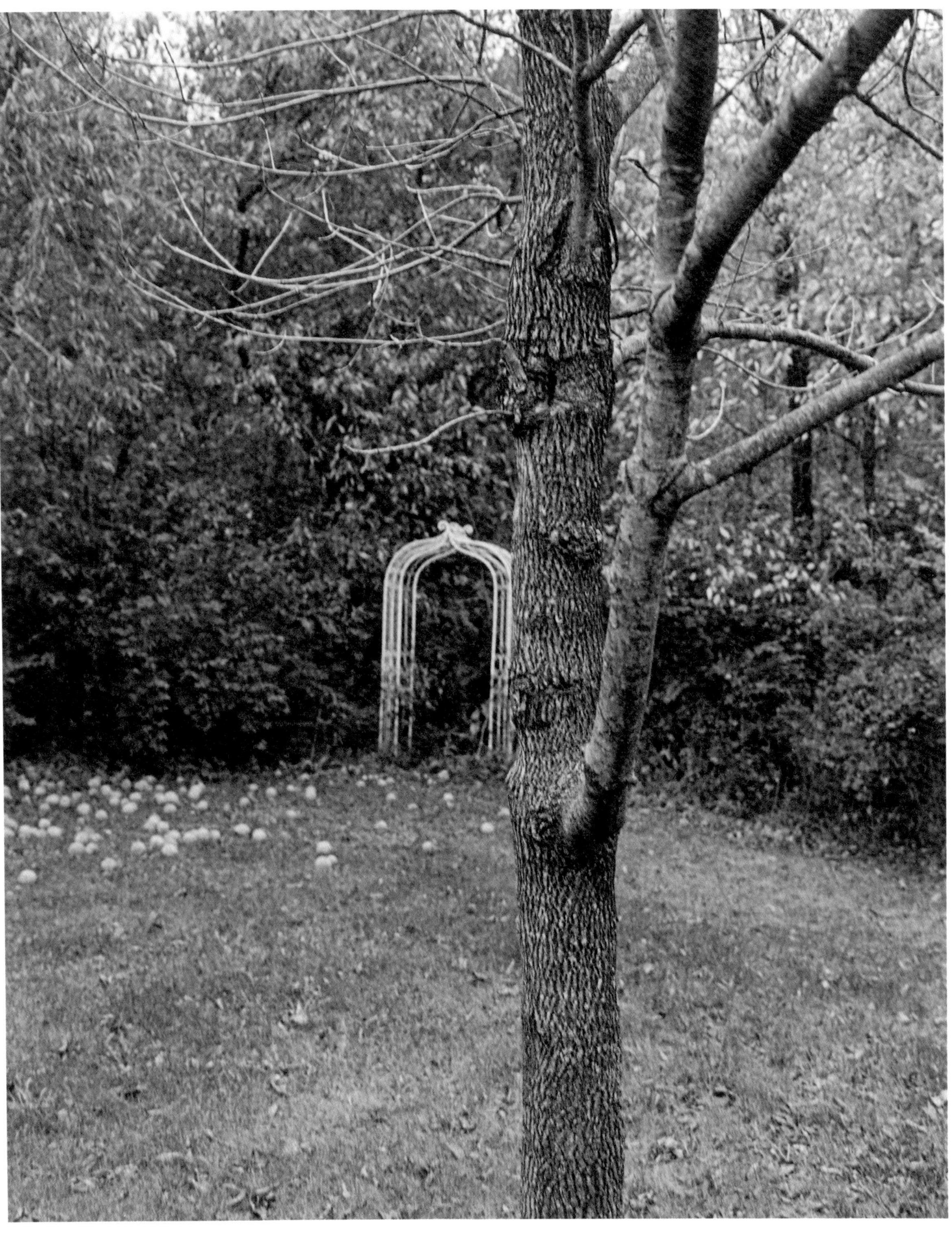

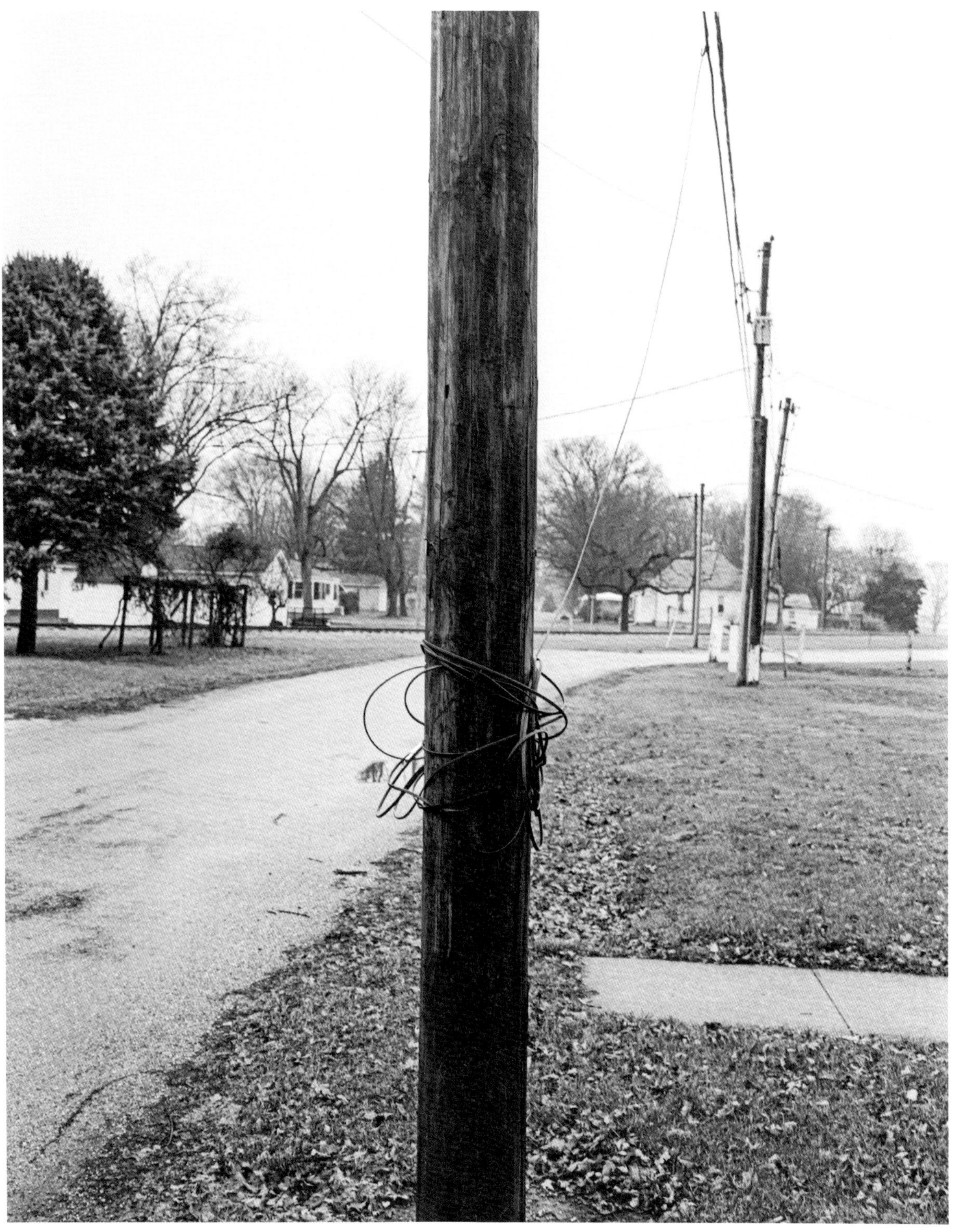

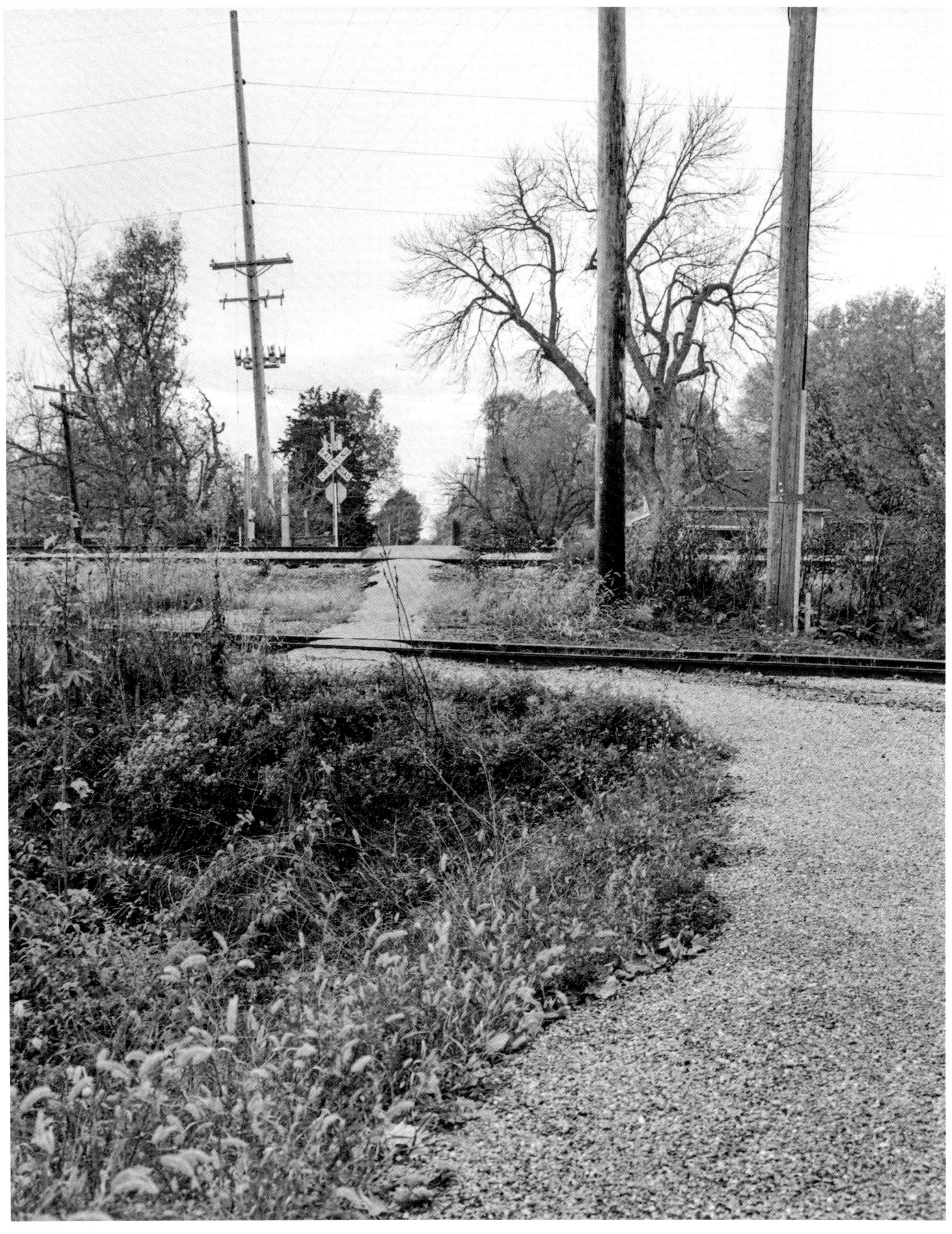